THE LEADER AS MARTIAL ARTIST

ARNOLD MINDELL,
Ph.D.

THE LEADER AS MARTIAL ARTIST

AN INTRODUCTION TO DEEP DEMOCRACY

HarperSanFrancisco

A Division of HarperCollins*Publishers*

Harper San Francisco and the author, in association with the Rainforest Action Network, will facilitate the planting of two trees for every one tree used in the manufacture of this book.

FIRST EDITION

Library of Congress Cataloging-in-Publication Data
Mindell, Arnold, 1940–
   The leader as martial artist : an introduction to deep democracy / Arnold Mindell. — 1st ed.
      p. cm.
   Includes bibliographical references.
   ISBN 0-06-250614-5 (alk. paper)
   1. Conflict management.   2. Leadership.   3. Social conflict.
I. Title
HM136.M53   1992
303.6'9—dc20   91-55333
                                                                CIP

   92 93 94 95 96 ❖ HAD 10 9 8 7 6 5 4 3 2 1
   This edition is printed on acid-free paper that meets the American National Standards Institute Z39.48 Standard.

Contents

Acknowledgments

Thanks and love go to Amy, who has lived and discussed every part of this book as it was created around the world. Her pioneering research on the transpersonal skills—or metaskills—of process-oriented psychology was a special aid to me in defining deep democracy.

Thanks to Julie Diamond and Leslie Heizer, who helped edit and correct the original manuscript. Important advice came from Julie Diamond, Jan Dworkin, Joe Goodbread, Leslie Heizer, Ursula Hohler, Kate Jobe, Dawn Menken, Pearl and Carl Mindell, Max Schupbach, Sonja Straub, and Nisha Zenoff.

Special thanks are due for the valuable suggestions and corrections given to me by Anne Marie and Constantine Angelopolous from Athens; Kerry Beale from Melbourne; Midi Berry from England; Steve Donvan from Big Sur, California; Yukio Fujimi from Tokyo; Moses Ikiugu from Nairobi; John Johnson from Washington, D.C.; Jeff Kelton from New York; Jan Loeken from Seattle; Alberto Melucci from Milan; Dayal Mirchandani from Bombay; Nora Montagu from Brussels; Joseph Pagano from Monterey, California; Peter Shikirev from Moscow; Thomaz Teodorzyk from Warsaw; Myrna Wajsman from Johannesburg; and Bracha and Ben Yanoov from Israel.

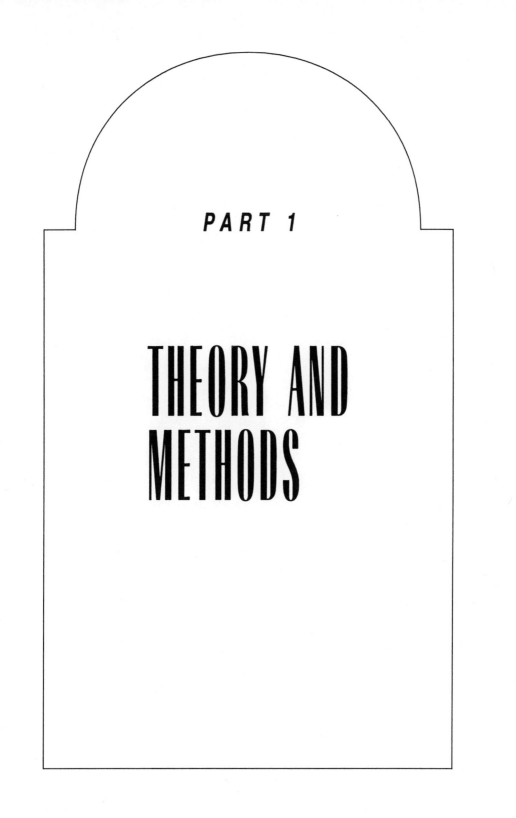

PART 1

THEORY AND METHODS

CHAPTER 1

The Eye of Turbulence

The following chapters describe skills, theories, and methods for working with our emerging world situation: a planet with five thousand different languages and religions whose inhabitants know more about launching spaceships than about getting along with each other. The vision inspiring these skills pictures a world that is home, one more captivating than war, safer and more meaningful than even peace.

As we enter the twenty-first century, we have the separate worlds of politics, psychology, spirituality, and physics. There are field theories, dreamwork and bodywork, relationship and transnational organizational work. It is now time to develop our "worldwork," a method that helps small and large groups of people to live, work, and grow together within their environment. We need worldwork that employs but is not limited to our knowledge of psychology, the sciences, and spiritual traditions. We need to develop a new profession that works with large groups as well as individuals to create a more meaningful and exciting world. Our new profession must put the older ones together and interact usefully with the environment and the physical universe and profit from the spirits of the times in which we live.

At present, the physics of matter and the psychology of people are more familiar to us than the atmosphere in which we live or the spirit of the times. What is this atmosphere or that spirit of the times? Is it tyranny or civil rights, a disembodied intergalactic ghost, or new archetypes trying to emerge into consciousness? Can we know this spirit and work with it, employ it to understand the stock market, divine future conflicts, or understand earthquakes? Our interest in these questions will determine the efficacy of the worldwork we develop.

The history of this book provides insight into its nature. After having studied physics and Jungian psychology and having developed process-oriented psychology, which works with dream and body connections within individuals, relationships, and groups, I accepted some of many invitations around the world to teach and work. During the course of this work, my wife, Amy, and I were confronted with many events that seemed at first to lie outside the range of our knowledge. What should we do with the large groups we were meeting? Was our process-oriented psychology cross-cultural? Was psychology a limiting name for our work?

I wanted to work better with the apparently unsolvable conflicts we met in Capetown, the murderous rage in Johannesburg, the anti-Semitism in Israel, the witch doctors in Kenya, and the street problems and religious ecstasy in Portland and Bombay. How should I facilitate the racial, ethnic, sexist, and gay and lesbian issues in our international and American groups? Could we develop something that was more exciting than war and also more sustainable than peace?

My new client, I dreamed, was the world. I wanted to focus on the group sensitivity of the Japanese, drugs and street problems in Portland, depressed organizations and failing businesses, the emerging enthusiasm and questions about democracy in Warsaw, Prague, and Moscow. But I found that my beginning worldwork skills worked only when I was inwardly at peace, and this peace is far easier to talk about than it is to genuinely attain when bathing in a sea of outer violence and conflict.

The implicit assumption that the group facilitator should remain neutral during conflict inspired me to reconsider other unconscious assumptions. What are the political implications of Western psychology, organization theories, and spiritual practices? Are women and men treated equally? Many psychologies have implicit prejudices against strong or emotional women and moody men and assume that gay and lesbian relationships are neurotic. Therapists focus upon inner life and neglect the reality of politics and environmental sensitivity. Too few psychological and spiritual practices help us with our relationships. Instead they recommend "good" behavior that no one but a saint can realize in day-to-day life.

It is devastating to assume, as some Western therapies do, that certain races and myths are more primitive than others. And most therapists assume that the only conscious human beings are ones who think about themselves all the time. Such apparently "harmless" assumptions are so full of naive prejudices that it is not surprising that our Western therapies and group and organizational practices are not solving city and international problems. We need a new kind of worldwork that will be used in Africa, India, and Japan as well as in the West. Our challenge is to carefully develop organizational and conflict resolution skills so that they reflect democratic principles and are widely applicable.

Worldwork methods must not assume that the responsible facilitators and leaders are always centered. Process facilitators, group instructors, business executives, psychologists, politicians, and teachers are rarely in neutral or normal states of consciousness, even at business meetings. Worldwork must not be limited to inner peace or outer equilibrium but must apply to real situations where there are chaos and attack, transformation and conflict.

Although an artist must learn the methods of her brush and paints, it is finally her most special feelings that allow her to be a successful artist. Likewise, the tools of worldwork can only succeed with the attitude of deep democracy, that special feeling of belief in the inherent importance of all parts of ourselves and all viewpoints in the world around us. While worldwork is a set of tools that must be continuously updated as we better understand our planet, deep democracy is a timeless feeling. It is found in all perennial spiritual traditions, especially in the martial arts, Taoism, and Zen Buddhism. It is our sense of responsibility to follow the flow of nature, respect fate, energy, or in the Far East, Tao or Ki, and of our role in cocreating history. Deep democracy is our sense that the world is here to help us become our entire selves, and that we are here to help the world become whole.

Such a special feeling sense may well be the outcome of psychological growth, or may be simply given. Yet like spiritual abilities, deep democracy alone is not sufficient in dealing with world situations. Likewise, worldwork techniques become meaningless in the hands of those without the necessary inner development, without a sense of deep democracy. Luckily, this sense can be developed anywhere. For whatever we do, whether cleaning house, relating to others, driving to work, conducting business, politics, or carpentry, studying, or writing, we seem to use the world as if it were a workshop, a testing ground to challenge ourselves and one another to open up to everything in our inner and outer universes.

Deep democracy is based upon those perennial psychologies and philosophies that include global, egalitarian approaches to personal problems. It is any form of bodywork that encourages us to understand our feelings and movements as global spirits asking for resolution. And it is that type of dreamwork that realizes that images do not belong only to us personally. Deep democracy is found in relationship work when we consider not only what we are saying but also what our bodies are doing. And deep democracy occurs in groupwork when we notice how group and political conflicts are connected to the spirit of the times.

Today, world problems and politics are not for only the rich or educated to solve, any more than organizational development is only for business. On our magical little planet, where the atmosphere can no longer be controlled by scientists, politicians, priests, or witch doctors, the world situation is everyone's task. We cannot afford to leave it to others. The time is ripe to develop a worldwork that connects transpersonal experiences with mundane reality, spiritual service and political activity, Eastern selflessness and Western rationalism, dreamwork and bodywork.

My background, which began with physics and Jungian psychology, now includes a lot of experience with large, turbulent group processes. I have worked with highly structured organizations as well as with loosely defined networks. I have experience with international business and racial conflicts in many global hot spots. Yet no amount of personal experience can suffice for our topic. Not even high-tech, quantum physics, and politics combined with inner development, awareness, and telepathy are enough, because our present world development is no longer under our control.

Individual Responsibility

If the world is a mixture containing our objective and subjective experiences, then worldwork must deal with outer reality by beginning with our inner experiences of it. Think of it this way. If the ground around a stone at the edge of a cliff gives way, the stone will certainly fall because of the force of gravity. However, if the earth under a person at the very same edge gives way, that person has a choice. She can sense gravity and choose to passively fall under its influence, or she can react to it by resisting and grasping at the edge of the cliff for life.

All of us are like the stone at the edge of the cliff. We are unconsciously pulled and pushed by the problems at home and in the world. However, we are only rarely conscious of our inner experience of these forces and of our ability to work with or against them. Since world history itself is also hanging at such an edge, the gravity of our situation weighs upon us. Each of us must notice it and ask, "Shall we fall or hold on?" Everyone notices the forces of our troubled environment and changing culture. To become conscious citizens of the third millennium, we must consciously react to these forces. Only then can we fully participate in history and contribute to transforming the times in which we live. This book is about our limited ability to cocreate our universe.

The forces that impinge upon us are described in part by physics, geology, and psychology. However, since our world is also a matter of human relationships, groups, cities, nations, and international events, these forces include the powers of dreams, body experience, family dynamics, groups, and organizational development.

Additionally, since our planet seems to behave in many respects like a huge living being, worldwork must deal with the living unity of groups and understand the world's mythologies and religions. It must create new cultures arising from the ashes of failed governments. The thesis of this book, however, is that worldwork can only succeed with democratic procedures. If we repress one part of ourselves, it will eventually overthrow our personal lives. No one can permanently repress the messages coming from sudden thoughts or body experiences without becoming ill.

Likewise, when creating new governments, we must learn how to listen to the voices of those we might neglect. A good worldworker is like the best therapist, a "democrat" merging psychology and politics. Democracy, in its simplest form of sharing power, listening, and gathering information, is the only sustainable form of governing ourselves, because no one likes being told what to do by others. Thus, dictatorial regimes can be only temporary.

Worldwork therefore succeeds only with democracy. But who is really democratic? Few of us listen to or are democratic with inner feelings unless personal trouble forces us to be. And most of us complain about our leaders, while giving them the power of dictators by avoiding public events and feeling weak. Even the simplest formula for democracy, including sharing and listening, cannot possibly work as a form of government without new skills, global psychological insights, and changes. This book speaks about these necessary inner and global changes, their connection to perennial wisdom, the sense of eternity and centeredness during periods of transition and chaos.

For worldwork to succeed, for the world to be able to gain access to all of its parts and really be whole, we need to develop. Some global theories and beliefs behind our attempts to organize groups propose beginning with people in reasonable states of mind. Angry people seem evil or chaotic according to these theories. The attitude of deep democracy, in contrast, must strive to develop a worldwork that deals with everyone, even those in violent emotional states and chaotic conditions, because these prevail during periods of rapid change.

It is my experience that human events that at first appear to be random and chaotic always evolve meaningfully from ordered, previously hidden parameters. Turbulent situations occurring during periods of rapid change or even revolution are full of potential meaning and order. Large group situations are analogous in many ways to personal problems. Physical illness, mental disturbances and insanity, and chaotic relationship situations are highly structured. Knowing how to find and unfold these patterns leads to the sense of stillness, the eye in the midst of global turbulence. Worldwork experience in adverse or wild circumstances based upon awareness of hidden parameters can make even the most pessimistic person optimistic about the future of the world.

Our world is like a field in modern physics. A field is an area in space within which lines of force are in operation. It is simultaneously everywhere with everyone. It is here and now in its entirety, whenever we merely think of it. The world is you and me. It appears in dreams and body problems, in relationships, groups, and the environment. And it appears through the feelings it creates in us when we are near sacred and awful places on earth.

Process Ideas

The process-oriented view toward the global situation says that the world has exactly those problems that we are meant to solve. They are just the perfect ones for us to grow with, and we are the only ones who can solve them. Governmental interventions by public leaders will never suffice without everyone caring for their own awareness and working together.

The central element behind all process work applications is the concept of nature, that the flow of even painful or difficult events such as illness, psychosis, or hate can become useful if we follow them exactly, compassionately, and with awareness. This process attitude is what Keido Fukushima, Zen master from the Tofukuji Monastery in Kyoto, means when he says, "Every day is a fine day." Every day can be made into a useful day if we meet it as our teacher. Then we have "no mind," or, more correctly, a free and creative mind, which can change with the movement of the seasons.

My original optimism about our potential for applying the ancient principles of deep democracy to modern worldwork problems was discouraged by the rigidity I met in institutional settings around the world. Implicit and explicit social codes, frozen traditions, rules, and the sheer power of organizational frameworks always seem to block awareness of conflict and the possible meeting of differing viewpoints. Furthermore, the unequal distribution of wealth and material and informational resources makes the ideas of harmony, peace, and institutional democracy seem like a naive American ideal.

These difficulties made me doubt and rethink my own assumptions, theories, and methods. Now I feel that only a few people in a hundred at any one time are required to achieve the attitude of deep democracy and use worldwork tools. Any other assumption at this point in history seems unrealistic. Thus, the following book is not based upon the naive assumptions that partners in conflict must share the same abilities or awareness or that they must even agree upon the existence of conflict or the method for working on it. The methods described in this book do not require equal or common social, cultural, material, or political ethics or frameworks to be applied.

As I began to write this book, I was constantly plagued by the following questions.

What are the skills we need to do worldwork?

How can we learn the heartfelt and intelligent manner needed to use these skills?

Can my ideas be used by my friends in South Africa, Japan, and India as well as in Russia, Europe, and the United States?

Am I sufficiently developed to write this book?

These were the questions that bothered me as I tried to make this work useful to people in Nairobi as well as San Francisco, Tokyo as well as Moscow.

In my previous book on global issues, *The Year I,* I attempted to connect the ideas of physics with cultural myths about global fields from all over the world. This book is based in part upon the findings of the *The Year I* and accompanies it by focusing upon how to interact with the global field. Here you will find theories, innerwork, training exercises, and practical examples. In a way, it is a user's guide to global process work. This book has four parts.

Part I, "Theory and Methods," investigates basic field concepts.

Part II, "The Metaskills of Leadership," explicates the personal development necessary to do worldwork.

Part III, "Global Work," discusses problems found throughout the world: political issues, tribalism and racism, street violence, poverty, and sexism. Experiences in the United States, Europe, Israel, Japan, and East and South Africa are described in Part III.

Part IV, "The Possible Universe," discusses the connection between physics and awareness and shows how the latter could possibly lead to a reversal of time and global destruction.

The book also contains descriptions of tested, cross-culturally applicable conflict resolution procedures along with their limitations and applications to large community processes and businesses.

Finally, this book recommends a political platform based upon our drive for awareness, interest in growth, and love for others.

CHAPTER 2

Field Theory

I originally planned to write a "how-to" book, listing the tools necessary to work with small and large group situations. However, I realized that I could not do this without taking into account the uncanny and awesome nature of group fields, which permeate the world in which we live.

At the surface, the world seems to function like an immense business trying to make a profit, or like a nation or tribe in the midst of creating its own identity. Yet under the surface, being a citizen of this planet or a member of any one of the planet's millions of subgroups is like being a participant in an immense workshop. In fact, most of us act like typical workshop participants, looking to the leaders to be gods, to have political, spiritual, therapeutic, and emotional wisdom and strength.

Unfortunately, few leaders are capable of this task we assign to them. Typical citizens or workshop participants have many problems in pursuing their own goals, either in their group or within their private lives.

Occasionally, a passing great spirit takes up the role of leading the workshop. We find momentary heroes and heroines, powermongers and saints, maniacs and scientists, but few facilitators who are interested in or knowledgeable about helping us to become ourselves and develop our own leadership potential.

If the world resembles a workshop or conference, it should be one in which people cannot wait to join, to arrive at the meeting, and to work alone or with others. The world should be a thrilling place to be.

The present situation is just the opposite: no one wants to show up at group, community, or business meetings; some groups and nations are run by terrifying tyrants; everyone is afraid to speak up, and if they do, no one knows how to listen. There is a threat of potential violence in the air. Lack of self-esteem seems to have reached epidemic proportions, and there are very few elders capable of loving others, helping them develop in an atmosphere in which business and personal growth are one and the same.

I am a great supporter of transpersonal visions, of making the unconscious conscious, of reaching the optimum in human potential, but the first step in remedying the present situation is to realize that, like in a workshop, we all have arrived here to get the most out of life. This is the perennial message of spiritual teachings. Life is a hunting ground in which we are to find ourselves, an awesome, uncanny place, and a garden in which to grow.

However, in order to realize this vision, we have to find out how to grow and flourish. Though we have the tools and knowledge for transcontinental communication, we do not know much about interpersonal and transpersonal communication. To learn this, we need to be aware of what we believe and how we behave. In physics, beliefs about the world are contained in theories. So let us start with theory.

Field Theory

The following analogy from systems theory of organizational development helps explain our global atmosphere. Try to imagine an organization to be something like a huge iceberg.[1]

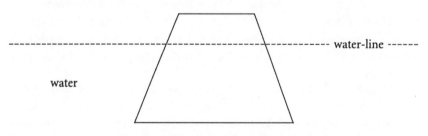

Organizational Iceberg

Imagine that your group, business, or nation floats in a sea or field, sometimes freely, sometimes connected to other groups and organizations. In the analogy, the leading people are placed high in the organization, above the water, and they look into the future in order to direct the iceberg's path, while the workers live below, supporting the whole group, usually out of contact with the directions and visions of the parents, elders, or leaders. Organizational development is based in part upon helping the whole iceberg work as a single unit.

When people have trouble with one another, the organization inevitably runs into trouble and may stagnate or decline. The organizational consultant then attempts to analyze the problems, diagnose the situation, and recommend solutions in which everyone becomes aware of the other parts. In this model of organizations, the sea represents interactions occurring between the organization and the outside world, including its possible parent organization, clients, and the material and information resources with which it must connect in order to exist.

The organizational development model works well for many situations, though some of its methods are based on the assumption that people behave in a mechanical fashion, like the parts of a machine. Against the clarity of this typical organizational dynamics approach, however, is another approach, one that takes into account the jungle in which we live, a jungle of inexpressible emotions, shadows, and unnamed forces.

Emotions and Groups

At any group meeting there are always invisible influences, which appear in the moods, motivations, group problems, and inflations, depressions, illusions, and dreams of its members. Moreover, organizations, like all groups, are riddled with internal jealousy, competition, love affairs, alcoholism and drug abuse, and subgroup battles between the scientists and bureaucrats, visionaries and middle-line managers, students and teachers, secretaries and bosses. When "after-hours" parties or get-togethers begin, these influences appear more clearly, as people drink in order to allow to surface the parts of themselves that had no room during the day. Now the personal problems, intrigue, gossip, conflicts, and sometimes even fights emerge.

Organizational development focuses not on the visions and dreams of the city, nation, or planet but on the immediate visions and goals of businesses and organizations, meaningful only for today or tomorrow. Think of Henry Ford's vision of affordable automobiles for the masses, Apple Computer's vision of a Macintosh computer on every desk, or Pepsi's vision to beat Coke!

These are visions with which to identify temporarily, but without the concept of the global workshop, without the knowledge of people's need to accomplish something meaningful in life, these visions are insufficient to keep the iceberg afloat.

In order to depict the reality of an organization, a new dimension needs to be added to the iceberg analogy. The diagram should also include the influence of the spiritual visions, emotions, feelings, moods, and even paranormal events that permeate group life. These invisible influences have been described as shadow energies in physics, as the collective unconscious in Jungian psychology, and as a morphogenetic magnetic field in Rupert Sheldrake's concept of the universe.

The new diagram would depict the disavowed, dreamlike feelings that create currents and undertows under the surface. Organizations are characterized not only by their overt and identifiable structure, purpose, and goals but also by their emotional features such as relationship conflicts, jealousy, and envy as well as altruistic drives, spiritual needs, and interest in the meaning of life. Existential and spiritual values, environmental problems, and battles in other parts of the world, though vaguely felt or rarely addressed, also structure inner and outer local events in an organization.

Field Characteristics

Information Float

Organizations are therefore not simply bodies, but dreaming bodies, physical entities moved by dreams as well as organizational structures, by emotions as well as spirits and money. The organization, together with its dreams and undercurrents, constitutes a field that is manifest in physical structures, human feelings, a particular atmosphere, and specific jobs and roles. If the field is congruent, then what a group believes and what it does are identical.

In most fields, however, what we do differs from what we say. This always leads to individual and group confusion, trouble, incongruities, and conflicts, whether the group is a couple, a family, a group of friends, a business, or an entire nation. The group is then submerged in an *information float,* a sea of signals that have impact, but their impact is disavowed.

As an example of an incongruent field, I remember working with a group of successful executives in a leading European country. These executives said they came to me because they wanted to work together and establish better working relationships, yet no one would speak up. They behaved in a stiff and frozen manner. It became apparent to me after working with them that their field had been made incongruent by an unspoken and unidentified pressure that each had to be smarter than the others. This pressure was part of the information float of this organization.

We shall speak later about how to work with incongruent fields and information floats in order to create a greater sense of community and team spirit.

Fields Organize Members' Identities

What is a *field?* Fields are natural phenomena that include every-one, are omnipresent, and exert forces upon things in their midst. In an example from physics, if you put a magnet under a piece of paper and brush metal filings onto the surface of the paper, then you notice the magnet's force field. It organizes the filings.

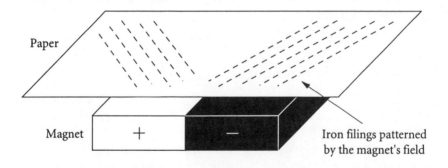

Paper

Magnet $+$ $-$ Iron filings patterned by the magnet's field

We think we manage or organize our lives and groups, but actually fields create and organize us as much as we organize them. Fields organize people into groups, if we understand a group of people to be any number of individuals who use the word *we* in the same way. Fields may not be visible to the naked eye, but they can be as pushy and as troublesome as an impossible spirit.

Obviously there are many different types of "we." The we of one group differs from the we of another in the way it identifies itself. A family is a group, since the members sometimes use the word *we*. Likewise, a bunch of bowling friends is a kind of we that refers to itself as a sports club.

There are businesses, cities, nations, religions, and races, and all these groups have particular patterns, agreeing on specific values and visions, even if these are not explicitly stated. Everyone in a group is connected by the same beliefs and values.

Hence, a field expresses itself in its beliefs, which create individual and group identities. Even though a field is invisible and much larger than the people it moves, it manifests itself quite practically in our beliefs. We experience our values and visions as pressing us to do certain things, and we sense these values as grouping us together, creating identities.

Fields may be invisible to the naked eye, yet they appear in the dreams of individuals, in the stories people tell about their groups, and even in the myths of nations. Individuals and groups are the battleground for the characters in the myths to complete their mythical conflicts. It is this dreamlike nature of fields that makes it so difficult for ecologists, economists, and politicians to deal with the world, because it is only partly organized by causal influences. The world is also organized by noncausal influences, by the dreaming field, and we need to be shamans and visionaries as well as politicians and scientists to solve the world's problems.

Fields Have No Boundaries

Fields have neither an inside nor an outside but permeate everything, like electromagnetic vibrations, or an atmosphere that has no well-defined limits.

Whether we belong to a given group does not depend entirely upon our saying or agreeing to being a member of that group. We are part of a given we if the group's pattern is in or around us. Whether or not we belong to a group may have nothing to do with where we live or with whom we communicate. Groups, like the fields around them, depend upon shared dreams. "Insiders" and "outsiders" do not exist in field thinking. Everyone touched by a given field is a part of it.

Fields exist regardless of time, space, and physical separation. Not even a physicist can say exactly where people begin or end in space, nor can a doctor predict the moment of a person's death. We are as much like fields and waves as we are like bodies and particles! We consist of ideas, concepts, and feelings as much as we do of matter and substance. This is why the Taoist recommends that in order to be connected to nature, we should follow our inner feelings instead of the outer appearance of things.

This characteristic of fields has important consequences for how we understand ourselves. Terms such as *personal* and *impersonal, individual* and *collective, me* and *you, inner* and *outer* are relativistic terms without absolute significance. Every feeling, thought, movement, and encounter is simultaneously an inner and outer event. Thus, meditation or innerwork is a form of worldwork, just as world events are also personal ones.

Fields Can Be Felt as Forces

Fields are often visualized in dreams and visions, but they can also be felt as if they exerted force on us, like gravity. Fields can make us feel heavy or light. Acting like electromagnetic forces, they attract us to each other or repel us into separate spheres. We experience them as weak or strong nuclear forces binding us to our essence or allowing us to drift apart.

In Taoism, the field is experienced as the Tao, a momentary situation imagined since earliest times as a force running along *dragon lines.* These dragon lines are considered "creases" in the universe. If you try to move something outside of these creases, you encounter resistance. Zen and Taoist literature warns us to move along these lines of least resistance. Translated into field concepts, this means we must live according to both inner feelings and sensitivity to outer situations. Following the Tao is like surfing the edge of a turbulent wave.

We all feel these psychophysical fields strongly. We sometimes notice and react to fields when we say, "The air is so thick I can cut it with a knife" or "You can almost feel the tension between them." We all remember the atmosphere of the family in which we grew up. Some field atmospheres attract us, and others disgust us. Force fields are felt and experienced through our own emotions, for example, love, attraction, warmth, jealousy, competition, fear, and tension, and through polarizations such as racial conflicts, gender conflicts, and insider-outsider tensions.

Fields Are Multichanneled

We feel these fields through our own emotions such as love, attraction, jealousy, competition, fear, and tension. We also perceive fields through their characteristic tensions: racial conflict, man-woman issues, outsider-insider conflicts. We can also perceive these fields through the environmental, spatial, or physical features of places in which we meet or in terms of the natural world around us.

In other words, we perceive fields through a variety of senses and experiences: in our dreams, body experiences, relationship problems, synchronicities, in small groups and in the world around us. The multichanneled manner in which fields appear means that when we work with fields and help them evolve, we must do so on many levels: through feelings, visions, movement, innerwork, relationship work, and large group interaction.

Fields Have Humanlike Characteristics

The world field has been described since earliest times as a huge god or humanlike figure.[2] The twelfth-century Christians thought the world was the body of Christ. Hindus believe that we all live in the figure of Atman. The ancient Chinese thought the world came from the huge anthropos figure called Pan Ku. When he died, his hair became the trees, his breath the wind, his bones the mountains, and his blood the rivers. This ancient belief reappears today in our tendency to anthropomorphize the earth, calling it *Gaia* and *Mother Earth.*

If the world we live in is a humanlike being, then we are its cells, responsible for its nourishment and empowering its organs, head, heart, and feet.

Another human characteristic of fields is that they are potentially intelligent. Thinking that the world or universe is intelligent has gone out of style today, but earlier, people believed in the wisdom of the world's field. Early Christians imagined there to be an *anima mundi,* God's female counterpart, as the architectural intelligence behind the world. In India many people still imagine Siva or Vishnu to be the wise field that thinks and perceives. They believe that our capacity to see, hear, and feel is Siva acting in us.

Actually, fields themselves are not wise; they are *potentially* wise. While they have the potential to be wise, fields, like the rest of us, consist of a mass of unconscious abilities. Fields are like dreams: without our conscious appreciation and intervention, most of their wisdom may not appear.

Thus the body symptoms we feel only hurt, unless the wisdom in their messages is processed. The visions we have may only confuse us if we do not cook them and encourage them to complete themselves. Mass movements in the world are useful only when connected with the needs of the people. And the planet's troubles will not turn into something useful unless we all help them to do so.

Fields Are Dreambodies

The world is a dreambody, a dreamlike entity that manifests itself in a physical reality. Empirical evidence shows us that body symptoms, when amplified, mirror dream experiences. The geomancers of old worked with this dreambody aspect of the earth. They discovered the spots and lines of the earth where human dwellings and populations could prosper and flourish, and they developed their villages and cities accordingly.

Force fields are dreambodies in the sense that the world is a physical body impinged upon by invisible and in part immeasurable forces. It should not surprise us when many of our illnesses seem to connect intimately to fire and storm spirits, peaceful and gentle winds, forest fires and race riots.

Fields Evolve

The whole world is constantly in the midst of immense changes. Even though most of us are surprised by geological changes or variations in the weather, we should remember that the earth is not a static being but like us, lives, dies, and transforms.

Fields evolve; they are not static or permanent but change and transform, analogous to weather. The fog drifts in, floats around, and may burn off or transform into clouds. The clouds may scatter, coalesce, change into harmless white powder puffs, or mass together as a dark and threatening storm. In a field, the feelings and ideas change and transform. Sometimes they stay hidden in the background, and other times they push themselves into the foreground. One example is in the changing shape of socialism in Eastern Europe.

In their development, fields becomes polarized, form parts, conflict, burst asunder, tear up relationships, and isolate us from old friends. But just as change and differentiation can be painful experiences, they can also pull people together unexpectedly, creating unity and peace between groups and individuals. What about the world field today? Where is it heading? What transformations are occurring? Will it blast apart in an ecological holocaust? Or will the creative new groups forming bring us together as a kind of planetary family that has never before existed? Will we create a new world before the old one dies?

Thought Experiment

Think for a moment about the possibility that fields cross time and space without walls. Have you ever found yourself working at a project by yourself and suddenly discover that others were doing something similiar without any communication between you?

Take a moment and think about yourself and the groups to which you belong. Imagine a group of which you are a part. Can you think of it as a field, as a huge humanlike being or divine figure? What role do you play in the humanlike creature? Are you the eyes, head, feet, or stomach?

Now imagine that the group is some huge anthropos figure, and you are being used in order to allow this creature to live. Your feelings, perceptions, reactions, and thoughts are necessary to this system in order for it to exist. The work you do is done in part for the figure. The field may be using your eyes to see with! How does this last sentence change your relationship to this group?

NOTES

1. From "The Organizational Development Iceberg," a lecture given by Kerry Beale at Eigenthal, Switzerland, April 1989.
2. See Mindell, *The Year I.*

CHAPTER 3

Timespirits

At about 7:30 P.M. on August 3, 1990, my wife, Amy, and I were completing a conference on addictions. We had encouraged our group of about two hundred participants to engage in a group process, by which we meant that the group should notice and process whatever was in the field. After many different individuals had spoken about what they sensed in the field, a teenager in the group who had apparently fallen asleep suddenly awoke with a muffled scream. It startled us all. Instead of neglecting this shocking disturbance, there was a consensus that this must be part of the field in which we were living, and so a small group decided to give greater form to the young woman's cry.

Within minutes, we had moved all the chairs out of the way, and two groups of people spontaneously formed. There were those who tried to give more form and support to the teenager's scream. This group yelled, screamed, and created havoc and upset. Simultaneously, the other group was incensed and outraged by the noise and insensitivity of the noisy group.

As the two groups became polarized, the situation escalated. The noisy group became louder and louder as the quiet group become more and more inhibiting. Then the two groups became aggressive and belligerent toward each other. At the height of the escalation, just as it looked unsolvable, I recommended that the group members feel free to hurt one another. At that moment, the people quieted down. Participants were silent for a moment, reflecting on how close they had just come to being violent. Some stood up spontaneously and began to express their individual feelings about what had happened. It is difficult to convey the drama of that particular evening or the way in which it resolved itself. It was, as many group processes are, a powerful occurrence and a moving resolution.

The reason I am telling the story, however, is because that very evening, on the other side of the world, Iraq invaded Kuwait, tilting the world toward world war. Could there have been some noncausal connection between the astounding conflict in our group and the world scene? Later in the book I will discuss such noncausal connections between group processes and world events.

Here, I must ask an unanswerable question: what creates tensions and conflict in the field? One view is that fields are generated by people's differences and polarizations. Just as the lines of force seem to be generated around the poles of a magnet, many aspects of our earth's field seem to be created around human differences, conflicts, and peak experiences.

A second view perceives the field as the prime cause of events on earth. The field influences relationship issues, earthquakes, and thunderstorms. What comes first: our conflicts or the field in which we live? There are times when we sense the field generating the issues, as in the conference mentioned earlier, and then there are other times when the issues seem to generate the field.

In many parts of the world, human problems are understood to be a consequence of force fields and spirits and therefore require the work of shamans to be healed. In many parts of the modern world, problems are believed to be generated by people. If we perceive the field as being the primary force behind all things, we develop shamanism. When we feel our personal moods create fields, we develop psychological explanations.

Thus, shamanism and psychology are complementary ways of dealing with life. Both explanations are necessary; one without the other is one-sided. Worldwork attempts to put the two together by accepting the nature of individual experience as potentially necessary and useful for the individual while avoiding the questions as to where this experience comes from and what causes it.

In fact, most forms of process work operate without the person knowing the origin of the events in question. We may ask questions about cause and origin, but for the most part the answers do not do much to alleviate the problem. Therefore, my conclusion is that the best we can do is to learn how to deal with events as they occur.

To work with a field, we will need a neutral vocabulary to describe events. *Tao* is a good word but rather vague and general. *Spirit* would be better, but its connotations are different for everyone. *Yin and Yang energies* are one way to describe polarizations in a field, but these terms are culturally biased. We could speak simply of *polarizations* and *group roles* to describe the structure of fields, but these descriptions are static and do not sufficiently emphasize the changes through which each side goes. If we use terms that imply stasis and immobility, then stasis and immobility will occur when we try to facilitate global processes.

We need new terms for opposing energies, polarizations, and roles. We need a term that implies that polarizations are not entirely a product of given individuals and groups and that roles are not static but rather change, escalate, diminish, and even disappear with time. For lack of a better term, I am going to refer to the aggressive and the peace-loving polarities in the above-mentioned conference as *timespirits*.

Fields seem to be troubled by relationships between timespirits. Any polarity or tension between roles and poles can be seen as tension between timespirits. Even the names mother and father are names for timespirits that are specific to a certain time and place and that change with time. Group fields are often polarized into conflicts between competing leaders, between insiders and outsiders, between followers and critics, and between women and men. Educational fields are polarized into teachers and learners, while political fields are polarized into liberals, moderates, and conservatives. In businesses, too, we inevitably have bosses and workers, insiders and outsiders, innovators and the establishment.

Timespirits are often experienced as mythical beings. Just look at how the media describe national fields and figures. Heroes are often given superhuman attributes, while the "bad guys" are linked with villains, monsters, and evil. There are fools and sages, starving people, and a great mother figure. Every field has a villain and a hero fighting for liberation.

At the center of social life lie a multitude of turbulent, conflicting fields that are structured by tensions between minority and majority groups, between the rich and the homeless, black and white, police and drug dealers, and countless more. Severe tensions exist between majority and minority timespirits in groups all over the world. We are constantly reading about struggles between races, ethnic groups, the sexes, religious groups, and classes.

The minority is a timespirit experienced by blacks in many places, by gypsies in Europe, and by Jews, among others. Wherever we look, we find a majority that rejects a given minority. All over the world, regardless of the country, any majority group will say the same things about the minority groups. Typically, majority groups or those in power believe that the minorities or those without power are

- different, strange, and dangerous
- stigmatized, morally inferior, or at least morally alien
- not deserving of social rights
- incapable and worthy of only the lowest social jobs
- unclean, evil, corrupting, or destructive to the world
- unconscious and dumb
- paranoid and belligerent
- intellectually inferior

Projections and Processes

The above beliefs about any given minority group, regardless of its race, religion, or sex, are universal. When we are inside these polarizations, we feel that these are human problems, created by people. But the minority-majority conflict is a conflict organized by a field; it is a timespirit dividing people from one another.

A common approach to the beliefs about minorities is that one group projects negative attributes onto another; projections are the negative parts of oneself. One should recognize that these are indeed projections and should finally withdraw them. People with this approach believe that withdrawing projections will improve relations between the groups. Withdrawing projections is obviously very important, and if one person or side does this, problems can be rapidly resolved.

But often negative projections are recreated or return after they have apparently been resolved. Certain conflicts seem to recur as if they were created not by people but by timespirits. Thus, withdrawing projections is only one part of worldwork; we must also process field tensions as if the field itself were trying to express itself. Worldwork approaches conflict in a group as an attempt by the timespirits to confront, conflict with, and know one another. In this case, individual human beings may feel as if they are channeling or being used by the conflicting field spirits.

Roles and Timespirits

The global field has neither an inside nor an outside; thus the momentary roles we feel compelled to occupy in a local field are simultaneously connected to global events. The atmosphere of our world or spirit of the times influences our bodies, tugs at our relationships, and polarizes, separates, and unites us with friends and family members.

The roles that we play in a group field are 'Zeitgeister,' spirits of the times, or global timespirits, as I call them. Timespirits are actually differentiated parts of the overall global field; they are roles found throughout the world: communists and capitalists, workers and managers, poor countries and rich countries, heroes and villains, and so on.

Elsewhere[1] I have used the term *role* to refer to the different parts of a given field. The term *timespirit* is an update of the role concept; it describes and emphasizes the temporal and transitory nature of roles in a personal or group field better than does the term *role*. *Timespirit* is meant to remind us of the transformation potential of the world around us.

Timespirits are like figures in our dreams. They are like whirlpools or vortices in an otherwise invisible field; they attract you, suck you into their swirl of energies. When you identify with a timespirit in a given field, you actually experience the emotions of that spirit; your consciousness is altered, so to speak. You get angry or become inflated. You feel heroic or victimized. The timespirit's energies make you moody and possessed, crazy and joyous, depressed and suicidal.

Transforming Timespirits

These descriptions, however, are not static or permanent states or oppositions. If one processes these roles by consciously identifying them, playing them, or even temporarily becoming them, they change. Timespirits transform.

A person or role that seems at first to be absolute evil may reveal more depth and compassion than we would have otherwise thought if that person or role is processed. Likewise, a puritanical and moral person could also transform rapidly into the essence of an evil or tyrannical figure.

Even though we describe timespirits as static, immutable constants, in practice they transform, change, and can surprise us with their capacity to yield, develop, and evolve. The villainy of an individual or group can soften and become benevolent; the good can become rigid or even tyrannical. The weakling can turn into the hero, and the nasty critic may transform into the wise teacher.

We all fear timespirits because of their capacity to possess us in both collective and personal settings. Everyone is aware of the sudden and potentially devastating effects of mass hysteria. Suddenly, we are sucked into roles and become irrational and unconscious. The less we know about ourselves and about the field's timespirits, the more easily we fall into altered states of rage and depression, ecstasy and paranoia. Because of their influence upon us and because we think they are permanent entities incapable of change, we fear these states.

We also fear timespirits because we identify the people filling the roles as timespirits. Groups and individuals, however, are not identical with timespirits; individuals have the potential to have many different feelings and timespirits within themselves as well as the capacity to become conscious of those feelings and timespirits and to use them profitably.

For example, haughtiness and arrogance is a timespirit that not only nonblack people can occupy in a field of racial tension; blacks, too, can temporarily occupy that normally "white" role in the field. Likewise, any group, black or nonblack, may suddenly find itself being the rejected or oppressed minority timespirit. We are different than the roles we occupy in a field. We are too complex, too multifaceted to be in any one role, even if a timespirit possesses us temporarily. I am sometimes a Brahmin, sometimes an untouchable, sometimes black, sometimes white. Sometimes I feel like a Jew or a Christian, and sometimes I am a nonbeliever or a fundamentalist.

There is something familiar but also unconscious in the way we identify people with static, absolute roles. We divide ourselves rigidly: you are the leader; I am the follower. You are white; I am black. You are European; I am American. You are Zulu; I am Bantu. You live on this side of the street; I live on the other side. You are part of the higher caste; I am part of the lower. We easily forget that it is the timespirits themselves that press us into roles.

When we process our experiences, they change. As we consciously experience the feeling of haughtiness or rejection, of anger or hurt, of sadness or need, the timespirit we occupy begins to transform. As timespirits transform, it may also happen that the antagonist becomes indistinguishable from its opponent. Where we had two parts in opposition, we suddenly have unity!

It is the tendency of people timespirits to change that creates community. For example, in the conference described at the beginning of this chapter, only when the aggressive and loud people expressed their wildness, and only when the quiet group was allowed to resist and become belligerent toward the noisy group, could the aggressive and conservative timespirits transform. The timespirits transformed and eventually dissolved, leaving only individual people, speaking from the heart, in the room.

I think of my own travels. After living for twenty years in Switzerland and then returning to the United States, having traveled around the globe, I wonder who I am. Am I European or American? Am I Japanese or African? Any one identity feels too rigid for me. I can no longer identify with only one timespirit in the field. I sometimes feel embarrassed and misunderstood when people ask me where I live, where I grew up, or when and where I was born. One day I feel like a global citizen, the next day like an American, and the next day like a peasant farmer from Switzerland.

Fields must exist, because every place I go, I find myself in the same place. Every town has a "Ned" who works in the hardware store, or a "Charlie" the realtor who winks and waves as I walk by. There are always a "Monica," an easygoing, wise, and thoughtful woman, and a "Herr Stoffel," the village leader. Though every place is different, unique, and unlike any place else, there is also a hologramlike similarity. Timespirits are spaceless.

Spacespirits

Though I speak about timespirits for the sake of simplicity and generality, in specific localities a timespirit cannot be thought of as being independent of the place. A timespirit may also imply characteristics of a given locality. Thus in given areas we must also consider *spacespirits.*

For example, there is a Los Angeles spacespirit, a feeling of the place, a combination of the weather, the wide boulevards and feeling of wealth, poverty, the smog, the mountains, the presence of Hollywood, and the beach and beautiful people. This spacespirit is much different from that of Bombay, with its crowded, narrow streets, beggars lying on the sidewalk, busy marketplaces, and mosques.

In earlier times, people paid more attention to spacespirits, but today we expect our architects and city planners to create the atmosphere of a place. Nevertheless, we are all sensitive to spacespirits, and, like indigenous people who identify certain areas, forests, and mountains as having more or less power, we are attracted to or repulsed by places and intuitively feel those "places of power" as areas that can either support us or make us ill. Don Juan, the Yaqui shaman who instructed Carlos Castaneda, speaks at length about these places of power.

Don Juan also stressed the transpersonal nature of allies. Allies are beings that take the "man of knowledge" beyond himself into other worlds. The woman or man of knowledge had to wrestle these spirits to the ground before the spirits could whirl them to death. The successful warrior who did so had then "tamed" these allies. Timespirits and spacespirits are potential allies, capable of helping us to transform the world.

Working with potential allies or spirits in this shamanistic way was only one part of Don Juan's contribution to worldwork. Whether he was dealing with warriors or with allies, Don Juan showed that part of appreciating life on earth meant using it as a hunting ground for "personal power," for discovering our own total capacities as individuals by working with ghosts and people, shadow energies and group situations, parapsychology and physics.

Individual work in the world needs public, group work to support it. The groupwork that we are all capable of doing is to realize that world problems such as racism, unbridled aggression, and insensitivity to others and to the earth are timespirits that flow beyond the cities and countries we hear about in the news. Timespirits are everywhere, inside and outside us, waiting to be dealt with.

Field Exercise

1. Think about a group meeting in which you have taken part.
2. Remember the atmosphere of that meeting. Imagine that the different parts or positions taken at that meeting were figures or timespirits. For instance, there could have been rebels and conservatives or leaders and followers.
3. Were there other timespirits present that were difficult to identify? Were there timespirits that were only implied or felt? For instance, were people afraid to speak up? If so, was it because of an unspoken critic or judgmental figure in the air?

4. Now that you can identify some of the timespirits that structure the field, how would you choose to make this field clear to others?

NOTES

1. See, for instance, Mindell, *The Year I.*

CHAPTER 4

Field Interventions

L iving in a group can be a painful experience. How many times have we wished that we could just disappear and withdraw from our relationships: family, school, business, friends, or even country? There are many reasons for the difficulty we have in living in groups, but one of them must certainly be the tendency for conflict and chaos to arise in them.

Dealing with conflict and using conflict resolution methods are most effective with people in reasonable, rational states of consciousness, but how can we deal with highly charged, emotional, rigid, or even violent groups? Almost any bargaining, negotiating, or conflict resolution procedure will work when people have already agreed to work on conflicts with one another. But how do we work with a group in the midst of turbulence, violence, ecstasy, or insanity, where no one wants to solve anything?

Turbulence and Self-Balancing Attractors

The concept of a field comes in particularly handy when dealing with a group in intense conflict. The best thing to do in a chaotic situation is to remember that we live in a field, because knowing that we are dealing with a field will organize how we work with turbulence and chaos.

My first belief is that the world we live in is a global workshop. Everyone behaves at one time or another as if this were the time and place to develop unknown sides of themselves and to realize and live their entire potential. I have come to believe this because the vast majority of conflicts I have witnessed become contentless after a certain point in the argument. The real struggle is the impulse to be powerful, win, love, and connect. This impulse comes from some unidentified place, some unknown timespirit or perhaps from the system or god we live in.

In modern physics, turbulence and chaos theory speaks of "attractors" that organize and make sense out of chaos, out of systems far from equilibrium. Attractors predict what type of order will appear in the midst of chaos. For example, in human systems, the drive toward balance, freedom, and harmony may be an *attractor* in our individual development. Just as all the loose stones on a hillside are attracted to the valley, and every pendulum will swing until it is still, the worst personal or group chaos tends, at least temporarily, toward resolution.

Fairy tales show many types of attractors that pattern our personal and collective processes. Regardless of what fairy-tale figures are involved, most stories tend to resolve their issues. Heroes battle the evil one in the name of the princess, and the prince awakens the princess from her witch-induced sleep. Likewise, all communities strive to maintain their highest visions against the banal circumstances of everyday life, and tenderness and love struggle to prevail wherever jealousy, hatred, and murder seem to dominate. Is the universe itself like each of us, trying to know itself, come together, and achieve some form of peace, harmony, and balance?

A system's tendency to balance itself can only partly be explained through causal reasoning. Change is also an incomprehensible, complex phenomenon; we have no way of knowing what creates change or when it is to occur. Change may also happen in one part of a field without any conscious communication to the other parts. For instance, the conflict in the large group process on the eve of Iraq's invasion of Kuwait, described at the beginning of Chapter 3, is an example of a noncausal field effect. Albert Einstein would cite the principle of nonlocality, which says that no locality can be identified independently of another; C. G. Jung would speak of synchronicity, and Rupert Sheldrake of morphogenic resonance. We could just as easily call it chance, the Tao, or a miracle.

Fields Are Self-Balancing

The tendency for systems to balance themselves and reach equilibrium is thus an *attractor*. In Chinese philosophy the female energy, Yin, swings toward and balances the male energy, Yang, just as dissent follows agreement. The wise facilitator knows and accepts this attractor, the tendency in nature to balance itself, and thus uses this knowledge to allow processes to unfold. She waits and consciously appreciates this inevitable natural flow. There is a moment to act and work, and there is also a time for stillness and patience.

Since agreement and antagonism are inevitable, the leadership position in a group should plan on being opposed or attacked. In fact, the more entrenched the leadership position is, the more it must expect to be attacked! Even where the leadership position is benevolent, kind, and humanitarian, it must be challenged and face opposition. Even a harmonious and balanced system must have a dynamic fluctuation between equilibrium and chaos if it is to grow.

Whether this self-balancing tendency is constructive or destructive, however, depends upon our ability to intervene in the evolution of our field. The self-balancing tendency of fields can also be a suicidal tendency. In its attempt to balance its different parts, a field can accidentally annihilate itself if no one is there to appreciate, unfold, and work with the polarizations, escalations, and deescalations of the field.

I remember a young boy who was suffering from a brain tumor. When I asked him what his experience of this tumor was like, he said it felt like a hammer on his head. He acted out the pounding hammer, and, to my surprise, the hammer banging on his head said to him, "Get to work and stop watching so much television!"

Based on this experience, I recommended that he drink black coffee, stop watching television, and get to work. In spite of his mother's and the doctor's objections, he followed my instructions. This intervention temporarily ended the conflict between his tendency toward laziness and his need to get down to work. Months later the tumor vanished.

The apparently malignant tumor contained the message of the hammer: discipline. The tumor was an attempt to balance the child's lazy tendencies, but it created destructive effects. Without awareness and skills to help our parts relate to one another, human systems will self-balance to the point of suicide. The same holds true in communities and nations. Unmitigated and unprocessed tension can lead to war just as easily as it can lead to the development of greater synergy and teamwork.

Wisdom and Self-Balance

Self-balance becomes wise in that special case when all parts are encouraged to express themselves completely. Only when explosiveness *and* sensitivity, leaders *and* disturbers are fully present and supported will a system usefully resolve its own problems.

There are several requirements I presently know about, and others still to be discovered, which must be met in order for wisdom to come from the self-balancing attractor. The first requirement is that we must be able to identify all the various parts and timespirits in a system. The second is that we have to allow them to speak.

All the parts in a field, even those we do not like or those we believe are useless, must be present and supported. Leaders and disturbers, macho behavior and sensitivity, insiders and outsiders, power and fear, criticism and support all must be present and identified in a given system. Some timespirits are more difficult to identify because they are what I call *ghosts*, implied or background feelings in the atmosphere. Ghosts such as jealousy, love, contempt, and dignity need to be brought forward and identified as well. Once all the parts are identified, they must be encouraged to speak. A system that gives no time or space to its ghosts will eventually be disturbed or destroyed by them.

Edges and Symptoms of Incongruity

Incongruity is the mother of tension and conflict; it is a sign of a system balancing itself. Incongruence means sending two conflicting messages simultaneously: for instance, speaking about peace and harmony aggressively but at the same time interrupting others. A group's problems are similar to an individual's problems. An individual resists becoming aware of his or her incongruities because doing so means looking at disavowed parts. Likewise, we are afraid to look at our group's incongruent communications because doing so implies that we might have to change and allow other parts to exist.

Communication difficulties and conflict between parts arise in the natural course of things and escalate because groups or individuals identify with only one form of behavior, one philosophy, or one part and negate the existence of others. All groups have *edges*, that serve to limit or define their identities. Edges may be experienced as resistances to recognizing, allowing, and living certain disavowed parts of the group.

For example, many groups have edges against expressing personal feelings in public. There is a tacit group agreement that personal feelings do not belong in the group. Some groups will prohibit aggressive and undemocratic tendencies. Others have implicit rules that members should not act childishly. All groups and organizations have beliefs, tendencies, philosophies, and behaviors that they promote and others that they disapprove of, prohibit, repress, or actively resist.

When groups forbid their disavowed parts, they become incongruent, rigid, and lifeless. Even when things are going well on the surface, background depressions and fears signal the decline of the group's life. People might be decent, nice, and moral to each other, but true communication is missing.

Groups may continue to imagine that they are successful while the outer world no longer supports them or buys their products. In an incongruent group, the connections between subgroups are tense, and teamwork is inhibited. Members stress the group's glorious past or make grandiose plans for the future, but no one works on the present problems.

The split-off and disavowed parts of the group come out in the group's gossip. All groups speak about other rival organizations, not realizing how these "other" groups are timespirits immediately present in their own field!

I remember when the Center for Process-Oriented Psychology in Zurich was formed. We spent quite a bit of time gossiping about another local psychological institution that was jealous of our popularity. We joked about their tendency to be overly organized and rigid, not realizing how much we ourselves needed more organization and structure at that time. We missed the timespirit of rules and regulations.

Awareness

Knowing about the structure, edges, incongruities, and self-balancing tendencies of fields educates us in perhaps the most important interventions in groupwork: awareness and waiting. If we are aware of what is happening, we can wait, allowing processes to unfold themselves and pointing out to the group what is happening. An awakened group will be self-balancing and wise.

Many conflicts, especially in small organizations, resolve themselves by simply being given enough loving attention by sitting quietly, understanding, and suffering each person's situation. Fields have the tendency to find equilibrium and resolve tension by themselves. But resolution requires the facilitator and as many participants as possible to be aware, notice what is happening, encourage overt and covert tendencies, and help others express themselves more completely.

Let me specify what I mean by awareness, as it has different aspects.

Sensing

The facilitator needs to sense the atmosphere. Sensing the atmosphere of a group means picking up and valuing the group's sudden and unpredictable signals and messages. These might appear in sounds the group makes, for example, angry voices, silence, giggling, or hushed tones. If you are the facilitator, you might notice the atmosphere of the group appearing in the feelings you have when sitting with the group: sadness, fear, apprehension, happiness. You should also sense the group's movements: when people get up and leave, when people are slumping or leaning back, or when kids are playing in the background. Perhaps relationship problems between members arise. These need to be appreciated and accompanied. Sensing the atmosphere requires us to reject none of our observations.

Sensing requires the facilitator to simply notice what it is like to be in that particular organization. Is the atmosphere pleasant, or is it uncomfortable and tense? What is the spirit of the place like? In what kind of a building does the group meet? What timespirits are present?

Addressing the Group Awareness

Share your awareness with others and challenge them to recognize their own awareness. Is the group in the right mood to work on its problems, or does it want to party? Do people want to work on their group experiences individually or through gossiping about them at home with friends? Are others in the group also sensitive to the atmosphere, or are you the only one?

Each group needs its own time, place, and rituals. There must be time for working and accomplishing things and time for self-reflection and discovery. Address the group on the topic of its awareness when the timing is right. Otherwise, whatever you say will be met with revolt. You can only successfully tell a group to do something the members are already thinking or doing. In my opinion, the best facilitators are not police but "assistants" and "enablers" who discover the direction of the field and share this discovery with others.

Sorting

Sorting means sifting through the feelings, issues, statements, and arguments of the group in order to identify what timespirits are present. One way to determine what is present in the atmosphere is to find out if there is a difference between the issues on which a group focuses and the feelings in the atmosphere. The facilitator can also ask the group what it would like to focus on and then sort out the important issues by noticing which issues elicited emotional responses, seen in such reactions as dead silence, giggling, embarrassment, or laughter. Such reactions indicate the presence of a *secondary process,* a background issue that the group has an edge against, an issue that it disavows. This minority issue is always the place where most of the energy is.

Use awareness to sort things out. Is the background issue in the group a conflict between women and men? Is it a feeling of being unsupported or undervalued? Is it rigidity in the management, boredom, or greed?

Identifying the Timespirits and Spacespirits

I have already spoken about the importance of identifying the various parts of the field as the basis for its wisdom function. A good rule of thumb for doing this is to guess that each timespirit has a complementary relationship to another part. For example, if people are loud or complain about being unheard, there must be a part of the field that is not listening. Unrepresented parts are ghosts; they spook the atmosphere and require attention. If a group feels victimized, it may not realize that a part of the field must be an abuser as well.

Objectivity and Neutrality

The facilitator must value all parts in the field, because in order for interaction and evolution to take place, all the parts must be present. Neutrality is more than not taking sides; it means realizing that no one person or event causes a group's conflict. There can be no assignment of blame, because no one part or person can be "bad" without the support of the entire system. There is no tyrant without a victim, no tension without people who try to avoid it! Neutrality and objectivity are important tools in groupwork because they also enable us to separate people from the parts or timespirits in the field. Each member is more than their momentary role and has all of the parts within himself or herself.

However, absolute neutrality and objectivity are Newtonian dreams, naive assumptions about ourselves. We know today from the new physics that absolute objectivity is not possible and from everyday life that we cannot step out of most situations. Therefore, we must learn to accept our limitations as participants in our planetary process and simultaneously discover how to facilitate that process. This will require special training and innerwork, on which we shall focus in the following chapters.

Switching Roles

Remembering that the people in a group are not identical with the timespirits will inhibit us from identifying a person with his or her momentary role in a group. In our individual lives, we pass through many stages of development. At one time we identify with one part of ourselves and at other times with another part. We are none of these parts, even though our individuation process enables us to gain access to all of them.

One of the dangers of unconscious groups is that they repress the development of the individual. Awareness of timespirits, however, turns group process into a chance for individuation. Individuals have the opportunity to discover the various timespirits in themselves. In fact, groups work best if individuals are aware of what timespirits they can identify within a given moment, move into that spirit, and give it a voice.

Switching roles is a group intervention based upon the individual's awareness of her own changing feelings in a group. Switching roles is recommended as a means for awakening individual awareness. Asking someone, "Are you in this role or another?" allows that person to become aware of the part he or she plays in the field. If switching roles is applied as a program independently of awareness, it becomes—for better or worse—just another implicit group game rule.

Group fields always polarize us into timespirits and hypnotize people into identifying with and becoming possessed by one spirit or the other. We thus become either heroes or victims, disturbers or followers. Awareness, if recommended and encouraged, however, transforms subtle but powerful group hypnotic pressures into a self-discovery process in which we notice who we are and how we change.

The best facilitators are assistants in human development; they are awakeners who gently encourage us to realize when we freeze in a role and lose access to the rest of our parts. Remember, the groups we fear the most are those in which the danger of being possessed by a spirit or complex is most acute.

A good facilitator will help us realize when we become incongruent in a given role, when other parts of us are trying to come up, and when we should be changing roles. But sometimes members get so frozen that they even need a physical touch to realize that they are no longer in their roles!

I remember an angry woman who once viciously attacked everyone in a large group. When the group finally defended itself, she reacted unpredictably by becoming incoherent and failing to react even as she was being attacked. She had become incongruent: her role as attacker had stopped because she no longer spoke to or answered the others. But she was still standing up in the position of attacker. What role was she in now? She apparently identified herself as powerful and could not make a switch to a softer position.

I suggested to her that perhaps the attacker role no longer fit her. I asked her if she wanted to step out of it. But she could not respond. She had apparently slipped into a trance, an unconscious condition. My guess was that she had been hurt by the group's reaction but did not want to show that.

I went over to her and gently touched her. She immediately began to cry and collapsed in a rumpled heap on the floor. She crawled over to the woman nearest her, who put her arms around her. This warmhearted scene was a dramatic and touching resolution to the group's process. I will discuss this powerful interaction later, but here I want to point out how we become attached to certain roles, in this case, aggression, and that awareness increases our access to other parts of ourselves and our group.

The Facilitator as a Model

Sometimes the facilitator must leave his or her neutral role and temporarily step into one role or timespirit in order to enable experiences to complete themselves. When the group is afraid of the experiences represented by that timespirit, it needs encouragement to complete them. At such a moment, it is helpful if the facilitator steps into the role and supports one viewpoint while encouraging people in other roles to step into the facilitator's role and watch over the group. Only by stepping into certain timespirits can a facilitator guess or read into the messages that are being sent by that role.

I remember a woman in a tense meeting in South Africa saying that she felt that she was the victim of the group's violence. Though there was a lot of tension, no one was overtly violent. The woman was speaking as a victim, but something did not seem congruent. So I went over to where she was sitting and tried to discover what her message was. As I mirrored her, I found that though she was speaking about being a victim, she was making strong and aggressive arm motions and speaking angrily.

I guessed into these movements, and as I spoke from her position, I added a tyrannical tone to the content of what she had been saying. I went beyond imitating her and said that not only was I a victim, but that I now wanted to get revenge and tyrannize others.

That realization brought about a momentary resolution. Everyone stopped arguing as the tyrannical role of trying to win and getting revenge became conscious. The feelings in the field changed from hatred to the sadness of having to hurt one another.

Edges

There are many ways to allow processes to unfold, but perhaps the most essential way is to *stay with the edge*, with awareness of the group's forbidden communication, its tendency to avoid emotional issues, personal feelings, idealistic visions, and relationship conflicts.

The issues against which a group has an edge will return if they are not dealt with thoroughly. For example, if a group member speaks about feeling angry or hurt, the others might become embarrassed or irritated and want to change the subject. If the group does not stay with the issue of hurt or anger, it will return until the issue is fully processed.

Weather Reports

Just being aware of edges is not enough. Once the awareness of edges and other phenomena is present, the great question arises as to how to share this information.

An enjoyable method of sharing awareness is to give a "weather report." None of us is completely neutral, but we can try to share our awareness of what a group is doing as if we were reporting on the atmosphere. The spirit of unfolding requires a curious, encouraging, warmhearted attitude.

I think of such awareness as group vipassana meditation. The weather reporter allows others who are focusing on only their personal sphere to know what is happening in the group as a whole. Everyone has a need to read the newspapers, to know the weather, to know the state of the whole world, not only the condition of our local areas.

A useful group process intervention is to simply state what is happening as if it were the weather:

Now there is a conflict in the center.

Now we avoid it. Is it too painful?

Now the conflict has turned into cold war, and no one is talking.

Now there is silence. Does this imply the end of the process?

Now a resolution has occurred, but a few in the corner seem dissatisfied.

Now everyone is talking and happy, and the weather reporter can go home.

Now we are beginning a new theme. How long shall we stay on it?

Now we are stuck and do not seem to get further. Have we missed an edge?

Now a community center is forming, and I must stop talking, because this form of awareness will destroy the feeling in the room.

Now we seem to be focusing on an individual. Is she representative of the group?

Now two people are fighting. Are they representative of our group?

Now there is tension between subgroups. Does this need to come out more?

Now something tyrannical is present. Is there a role for him? And where is the victim?

Now we stepped over a numinous, spiritual moment. Should we neglect it or go further into it?

Now I notice that there was an escalation. Let us take it further.

Now I notice the two conflicting parties separated a bit. Is this a deescalation? Should we experiment at this point with dropping the issue?

Now the argument is getting hotter. Perhaps there will be a murder soon.

Now our behavior seems to have shocked us. Some feeling is present.

This first meeting and confrontation were enough; why go further? Do your quiet voices mean that everything is worked out for today?

State Changes

When groups have been blocked for a long time, an immediate state change can bring great relief. There are various ways of bringing about such a change. The basic principle is to use a channel[1] or mode of perception and communication that has been neglected. For instance, a group that has been talking a lot may gain insight through movement. The facilitator can ask those who want to move to stand up and stop talking. As people wander around the room, a new process that had been suppressed by the dominant mode of talking may appear. People might break up into small groups and chat, hug each other, avoid each other, dance, or just take a break.

Some American groups may discover new aspects of themselves through being silent or making noises. One Japanese group we worked with profited immensely by being silent after a long discussion.

Sometimes a state change can be effected by letting chance determine what to focus upon. The members might spin a pointer (for example, a pen) in order to select a single person, whose inner, individual process, might be taken as a mirror of the group's situation.

Using divination methods is always surprising. Once a large group was arguing over some seemingly unimportant issue. The pen spun to a woman who had a bad conscience and guiltily admitted that she had just stolen something. The group stopped arguing, and all the members focused on the crucial issue; their feelings of neediness and poverty.

Rise and Fall of Powers

Frequently the state of a large group process will change without anyone consciously noticing. Even nasty, tyrannical timespirits can change. For example, two sides may have been arguing, but as soon as the emotions in the background come out, the fight ends. Even though the mood changes, voices become more quiet, and the tension drops, people continue to talk about the old issues because they have become attached to them.

A facilitator needs only to mention that the voices are quieter and that the mood has changed. We should not forget that great powers rise and fall. When they rise, we need to encourage them to come out, but when they fall, we should let them die.

Being Personal

Another important state change occurs when people begin to speak personally about the roles they have just been representing.

There are many levels to group process. One level deals with group issues and roles, and another level deals with our personal, individual feelings about the group situation. It seems that only when all the roles and timespirits have been expressed are groups ready to be personal. Being personal too early can inhibit the whole group from taking part in the process. Not being personal and genuine when the roles have lost their energy makes everything seem like a game.

Harmony Might Not Be Helpful

Harmony is a beautiful state, but it is not nearly as powerful as awareness. Some processes cannot be completely resolved, either because they need more time or because the group cannot resolve them; resolution needs to be done at the individual level. Total resolution might also be harmful to the remaining dissidents. Dissidents represent the future life of the group; they point to the next step, the growing edge of the group.

Guessing the Future

The hidden, disavowed processes found in feelings, symptoms, or dreams, always point to the next step for the individual and group. Thus, it is possible to guess the future from the secondary processes of the moment. For example, a group working on individual issues may have to work on relationship difficulties as its next step. Or a group that has become harmonious will probably bring up conflict at the next meeting. A group that has been verbally violent will undoubtedly search for quiet and sensitivity. A group that has avoided a topic will certainly have to deal with it next time. Processes evolve unpredictably, but they also have very predictable features.

Group Unconsciousness

Many people in groups or businesses are afraid to express themselves because they do not feel at home, fear being disliked, fear losing their jobs, or even fear being physically attacked for their feelings.

Probably most people, including so-called bosses, repress themselves in order to secure success. Everyone in the system contributes to the difficult atmosphere by being addicted to security and support. Such group fields breed dependency, belligerence, stasis, and eventually revolution.

In some situations fear may be processed by participants creating a position for it in the field. The facilitator can guess into the dependent role's feelings. Some of the fears and feelings that might be voiced are the needs for love, approval, support, and security.

Blank Access

Blank access is a term I use for an intervention that invites the hidden processes to appear. The facilitator asks a question or makes a statement virtually devoid of content, which encourages the others to fill it in. Statements such as, "Is there a certain feeling in the room that is not expressed yet?" or, "Was someone over there thinking something they were shy to say?" help the members bring out their thoughts and feelings without putting them on the spot.

A blank access can also be nonverbal. I once slipped out of the room during a fight in a particular group, went into the bathroom, put a black stocking over my head, and returned. No one knew it was me at first. They were in shock.

"Who am I? Project onto me," I said. The members imagined some wise being who knew how to resolve their conflicts. One after another, the members took over the role of the wise spirit and resolved their problems in minutes.

Teaching

Not every group wants to learn about itself; many just need help settling their immediate problems. But a group that is ready to grow in its own self-reflection will need a teacher as much as it needs a facilitator.

A wonderful and important moment for some groups and organizations is when the members take over the facilitator's job. The facilitator is just another timespirit. In fact, *facilitator* is no longer the correct name for this timespirit; *colearner* would be better. Each member of the group needs the opportunity to represent wisdom, to experiment with awareness, and to have a chance to change the world.

The following are exercises in awareness for those interested in learning how to enhance a group's awareness.

1. Edges in Groups

This exercise induces awareness in participants about the kinds of things they are generally too inhibited to express in a group. In groups of four people, find the group's edge by asking yourself:

How am I not feeling completely free in this group right now?

How is this conflict a part of my individual growth?

Within your group of four people, break into dyads and let everyone have a chance to work on these inhibitions and edges by role-playing the conflict between themselves and an inhibitor. Or the reader may now ask herself how she is not free in groups and then ask

What person or force is inhibiting me?

How can I respect this force and also be free?

2. Sorting Issues in Groups

1. Ask groups of four to bring up topics on which they would like to work.
2. Ask the groups to sort out the issues according to their "emotional charge," that is, according to which issues make impact and which ones make no or little impact.

3. Weather Reporting

Pretend you are a weather reporter and notice the atmosphere and emotional feeling of the group. Bring out what is happening in a group in a neutral and nonjudgmental way. Include in your reports to the group

the processes they like talking about and the spirits they seem to neglect the way they deal with emotional and spiritual topics

their tone: whether they are serious, playful, personal, or businesslike

4. Rapid State Changes

Practice enabling groups to make rapid changes by doing the following:

Change channels. Ask the participants to stop talking and to move, or to sit silently for a minute.

Invite people who are in conflict to interact physically and invite the group to create a practice environment in which this can happen.

Initiate conflict into a boring group through raising a repressed or minority issue.

Play out the role of a third party who is not present but is being discussed.

Notice deescalating tendencies in a fight and ask people to experiment with being quiet.

NOTES

1. For more information on channel and channel theory in process work, see Mindell, *River's Way*. For more information on channels in group process work, see Mindell, *The Year I*.

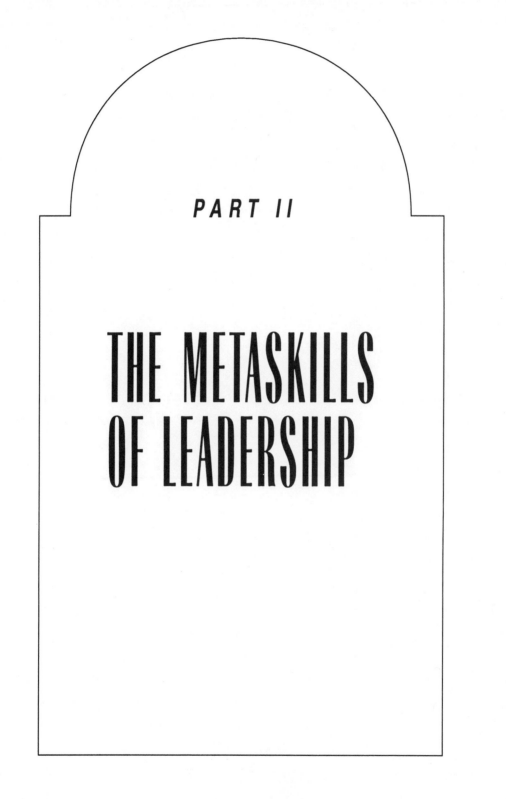

PART II

THE METASKILLS
OF LEADERSHIP

CHAPTER 5

The Leader as Martial Artist

When I learn to hammer in a nail, I have learned a skill, but the way in which I use the hammer is a *metaskill*. The same is true in developing skills in working with individuals and groups. We need to learn skills and techniques, but these cannot be applied without the proper metaskills of deep democracy.

In working with groups or organizations in serious trouble, either with themselves or with other groups, the decisive factor for the facilitator is not the skills or methods she uses but the attitudes she has toward the group. These attitudes and beliefs are what I call *metaskills*. They generate tools for dealing with any situation.

Think of compassion as a metaskill. A skill applied without compassion for people will have less effect then the same skill applied with compassion. This obvious simple truth is not so simple in practice. We all know how to teach skills, but metaskills are more complex. Metaskills are essential in doing worldwork, but how does one teach and learn attitudes, beliefs, and feelings about people? Discovering and developing metaskills require a mixture of talent, inner development, and outer role models as well as other factors that I have not yet identified.

This chapter attempts to outline some deep democracy metaskills for doing worldwork. I am still somewhat uncertain how to teach or awaken these metaskills in others. I can only admit my own beliefs, hopes, and motivations about people and try to discover what my own attitudes and metaskills are. I use the analogy of martial arts to describe some of the attitudes the facilitator needs for doing worldwork.

The Facilitator as a Role

Working with any group requires, first and foremost, awareness of one's role as a group facilitator. The facilitator role differs from other roles in a group in its interest in the well-being of the entire group and its relationship to the world. The facilitator does not belong to any given party or part, unless, of course, interest in the whole can be considered a part as well.

From the viewpoint of both group and personal psychology, leadership and facilitation together are only one of our aspects, one part of our overall process. In other words, leadership is not connected to any one individual but can be experienced in each one of us at some time. No one is only a leader! Knowing this is one of the crucial metaskills of leadership, for it allows us to be fluid and multifaceted as leaders and as followers.

Learning from the Group Energy

The majority of people deal with tensions in a group by one of three means:

repressing the tensions and trying to be nice to one another

analyzing the tensions and trying to change ourselves or others

getting into the tensions and hurting one another

The concepts and skills of martial arts offer another process-oriented way of dealing with conflict. The martial arts describe some of the attitudes the facilitator needs toward the group with which she is working. Aikido, especially, can be used as a new way to look at tension and conflict, perhaps even giving us a way to get over our fear and become involved in tensions.

Japanese Aikido is based on the principle of field energy, or Ki. In *The Spirit of Aikido,* Kisshomaru Ueshiba, quoting ancient Japanese texts on martial arts, relates Ki energy to metaphysical principles in China. According to Ueshiba, Ki

> was the source of creativity expressed in the form of the yin and yang (Lao tzu), the vital fullness of life (Huaninan-tzu), the courage arising from moral rectitude (Mencius), the divine force that penetrates all things (Kuan-tzu) (p. 21).

It was connected to "empty space," the "void" or "nothingness" (Lao-tzu), and the "formative energy emerging from chaos" (Chuang-tzu).

In our terms, Ki would be the field's force or intensity. Like the field of a group, Ki is empty or contentless. It is an energy that creates changing patterns out of chaos. Since Ki is the "courage arising from moral rectitude," it is also the metaskill or attitude necessary for dealing with itself. The field teaches the facilitator how to work with the field itself by remaining void, or open to the movement trying to happen.

If we want to ski, the mountain itself becomes our teacher and method. If we want to surf, then the sea is the teacher. If we want to learn how to facilitate difficult groups, nature teaches us the way through its changing seasons of anger and love, egotism and compassion. The best interventions for a group in conflict are not those that the facilitator brings in from the outside but those that arise naturally out of the group's changing moods, tensions, emotions, roles, and timespirits. The narrow path that the facilitator must follow is a path the group itself creates and can accept.

According to Ueshiba, Ki is a "divine energy." In my experience this means that the group's energy cannot be completely controlled or predicted, that it is a mysterious spirit. I have tried many times to govern the way in which processes proceed. Sometimes I have been successful, sometimes not. When I could not control a group process or intense conflict, I inevitably discovered that the reason was that I had turned against it and some of the people involved. I thought I knew better. Since I was not following the Ki, or spirit, I learned the hard way that my job was to serve and not to act like the spirit.

Self-Balance

Densho Chushaku, an important classical jujitsu text of the kito school, recommends that the warrior balance the overall situation by following the different forms of Ki and using the energy of his opponent.

> *Kito* means rising and falling. Rising is the form of yang, and falling is the form of yin. One wins by recourse to yang and wins by recourse to yin. When the partner shows yin, win by yang. When the partner is yang, win by yin.... To discard one's strength and win by using the partner's strength works because of *ki*.[1]

The drive to win is more disturbing than useful in worldwork. Most of the martial arts do not speak about fighting and winning but are concerned with the overall development of the participants. Occasionally, as in the above quote, the message is concerned with overcoming the opponent and winning a battle. The recommendation is to notice how the field balances itself.

The facilitator's job is to follow the Ki: the field's changing excitement, interest, and energy. The facilitator "wins" in groupwork by going with what is present. She follows excitement when it arises by giving way to it and follows depression when energy falls by revealing its essence.

I remember the tension once arising in a process work group when outsiders in the group felt shut out by more advanced trainers identified as insiders. Suddenly, during the polarity, everyone fell silent. I wondered if the outsiders had said all they felt. An outsider then said the insiders appeared inflated, as if they knew everything and were better than the others. I listened carefully to the attack, and as an insider (as well as facilitator), I realized the truth of the attack. After all, I myself, I told everyone, am sometimes inflated, blowing up like a balloon when I discover something I imagine others have not known, and then I go down like lead when attacked for being inflated! Everyone laughed as Yang was hit by Yin!

The facilitator uses awareness by noticing her own feelings, switching roles and identities, and moving back and forth so that she is neither attacker nor defender, but both in and out of the tension at the same time.

The ideal facilitator does not have a program but follows the Ki, or energy of the group. She helps complete the group's experience by using its energy and listening closely to all opponents. She may even assist her own enemy in completing his opinions and viewpoint. This type of facilitation is good ecology; it does not require additional energy to make change. The field will readjust itself and reach resolution if we use the processes that are already there.

Following Hidden Ki and Secondary Processes

Following the field is contingent upon recognizing the field. The parts in the field are often hidden or disguised. In *Heiho Kaden Sho* on the art of swordsmanship, it is said that "the Ki that is hidden and not revealed presents the opportunity for victory."[2]

Imagine a person who identifies with being angry but is really needy and sad, then the *hidden Ki* is sadness. Others feel this sadness, though the person may not notice it. Here, resolution of any communication problem depends upon following the sadness, the "double signal." A double signal is a signal containing two conflicting messages. For instance, in a group process, someone might be asking for help and unconsciously be yelling at the group for not working hard enough. The double signal, the hidden Ki, is yelling and needing help. The hidden Ki of a double signal is always that which the person does not identify as the main part of the message.

Find the hidden Ki as a facilitator by noticing when people are not just angry but also needy. Feed the need, not just the anger. When someone is criticizing you, notice if he is also shy about it, and address the shyness. Notice when your opponent is loud and in need of more attention, and listen appreciatively. Notice when your opponent is belligerent and also correct, and compliment the correctness. Notice when your opponent is not just powerful but also secretly hoping to be restrained. Help him by also complaining about your inability to restrain him. This is winning through the *hidden Ki*.

Love of Nature

In *Tengu Geijutsu Ron*, on swordsmanship it is said,

> In all matters related to the arts, including martial arts, superiority is determined through training and practice, but true excellence is dependent on ki. The grandeur of heaven and earth, the brilliance of sun and moon, the changing of the seasons, heat and cold, birth and death, are all due to the alternation of yin and yang. Their subtle working cannot be described by words, but within it all things fulfill life by means of ki. Ki is the origin of life, and when ki takes leave of form, death ensues.[3]

This poetic description of the Ki is more than a recommendation about following processes. This text implies that though skill or superiority depends upon training and practice in interventions, actual success depends upon our metaskills, upon perception, love, belief, and ability to follow the changes of the field.

This statement describes the heart of deep democracy in individual work and groupwork. Facilitation depends upon our respect and love for nature, the "grandeur of heaven and earth," our awe of the land and the sea, mountains and snow, the changing seasons and the changes in human beings. All of us are at heart nature lovers, but we often forget our love for nature when we deal with one another, thus dividing nature from humanity, the space spirits from group process.

We all too often try to solve problems without believing in the wisdom of natural flow. We wear ourselves out using our own energies rather than using only interventions that are recommended by the interactions between the timespirits themselves! Nature makes choice; we only need to follow.

Detachment

A central characteristic of leadership is the ability to maintain awareness in the midst of group chaos and confusion. Perhaps the greatest difficulty in developing this leadership characteristic is that it can only be learned "on the job," in the midst of group processes. The intense heat created by positive and negative projections, strife and celebration, anger and love disturbs the development of the leader but also helps her develop her abilities to completion.

Facilitating and leading relatively harmonious and peaceful group processes can be done by almost anyone, but managing tense public situations is a different story. It requires study, practice, and, above all, innerwork.

A classical story from Master Ueshiba, the founder of Aikido, describes his detachment. Master Ueshiba relates that while traveling he found himself in the midst of a battle.

> I prepared myself for death and then, saw clearly that the movements in martial arts come alive when the center of ki is concentrated in one's mind and body and that the calmer I became, the clearer my mind became. I could intuitively see the thoughts, including the violent intentions, of the other. The calm mind is like the quiet center of a spinning top: because of the calm center, the top is able to spin smoothly and rapidly. It almost seems to be standing still.[4]

The master was able to detach and avoid getting attacked. But how? I suspect that his "preparation for death" was the crucial element in the story. Fear of death can be a godsend. We can use our fear of attack as an indication that part of us should be annihilated.

Becoming aware of all of our parts, we can die, so to speak, before we are killed, and protect ourselves from attack. If we lose our self-importance, we become uninteresting as targets. We become invisible. If we remove ourselves, then the attacker has no one to hit, and the Ki or field can move us about as if we were enacting the dance of nature.

But avoiding attack is only the beginning. A next level would be to consciously admit and then step away from our one-sided position, become neutral, and thank our attackers for helping us loosen up our old identity. Then we could even take their side and help them complete their process. I will talk more about conflict in the next chapter.

But the question of how the facilitator is to arrive at her attitude of detachment still remains. Detachment is not always possible. The following are some hints for developing this important metaskill.

Burn Your Wood

You can be cool in conflict if you are not interested in the battle, but this can only be achieved if you have already fed the fires of your own rage. If you have already raged long enough about the issue being discussed in the group, then there is no longer any wood. The fire is done.

Being detached, however, does not mean that you are uninterested in the conflict; just the opposite—you have more feeling for everyone in the fight, including your opponents. Being detached only means that the issues are no longer burning ones for you.

Accumulate Experience in Conflict

Detachment sometimes comes after you have so much experience in conflict that you become detached from the forcefulness and futility of the attempt to win. You can appreciate and support others in their attempt to win without becoming infected by their way.

Accept Conflict as Your Fate

Sometimes you may realize that you are in a tense situation because you need to be. You see conflict as your fate. You cannot avoid it, so you make the most of it by learning and using it to grow.

An Example

The following example of group process and conflict illustrates some of the above-listed metaskills for facilitating conflict.

My wife, Amy, and I were conducting a workshop for approximately 150 participants at a residential center. We were visited one evening by part of the center's staff. The staff complained and criticized us for not following some of the rules of the center and for being sloppy. They complained that our group left glasses and dishes in the seminar room instead of carrying them into the kitchen. They were overworked and underpaid and were angry that the group did not pick up after itself.

Their point was well made; indeed, we were just plain sloppy. However, even when we admitted it, apologized, and promised to reform, the leader of the staff continued to attack us. We defended ourselves and complained that they were becoming unfair in their attack. A member of their staff admitted that they were under tremendous strain and were in conflict with one another. He suggested that their internal conflicts were the real problem. We offered to help them "clean up" their difficulties if they needed it. They agreed, even though their leader was still dissatisfied with us.

They thrashed out their internal conflicts, and it seemed as if progress had been made. Toward the end of the evening, one member of our group came forward and said she was still hurt from the staff leader's earlier attack. She asked the leader of the staff for an apology. The leader said she did not want to apologize and was not able to. The participant again asked the leader for an apology, and the leader grew even more adamant. As the situation escalated, I jumped in and got down on my knees in front of the leader and begged for her forgiveness. When my plea did not soften her, I rapidly changed and became furious!

I stood up and bombarded the woman with a barrage of criticisms. I stopped as suddenly as I had begun and took her side against me, feeling truly sorry that she had to take all of my criticism. She just seemed to freeze even more. I went over and physically took her side and tried to show her how to defend herself against me. Since she could neither attack me nor protect herself, I suspected that she was only standing in the same place but—as I mentioned earlier—internally had left her position. Hidden Ki!

I gently touched her arm, saying that she must have cursed the day she began to attack us and must never have suspected that such a scene would have happened. She collapsed on the spot, sank to her knees, and hit the floor. In a moment she came back to her knees, crawled across the floor, and, in a moving gesture, hugged the woman who had asked for an apology, and the evening was done.

The next morning, most of the members of my group were satisfied with the previous night's process, but a few were unhappy with what I had done. One man said he was angry at me for having been so tough with the staff leader.

The whole group got involved, and the conflict began again. Others in the group reminded the man that I had also been humble. I reacted by defending myself. I said that the woman's attack needed a well-intended response. I said that things had ended well, that I had also taken her side, and that I genuinely felt bad for her and wanted to help her out of her impossible position.

Again hidden Ki! Hidden behind the critical comments was also a request for me to listen closely, to encourage the speaker to stand up and speak his mind and to appreciate his leadership potential. Though I had been able to follow the Tao the evening before, I almost missed the Tao of the following morning because I did not realize that my new attacker himself needed recognition as a leader, and because I was simply insecure.

But there was another hidden Ki! I, too, was insufficiently happy with my work the night before. In retrospect I see that though I was happy with the resolution, I had repressed my unhappiness about having to fight in the first place! I felt bad that I had been so forceful with the staff leader.

I was obviously attached to doing well, because I was relieved when, two days later, the staff leader who had attacked us reappeared for a few minutes to humbly say that her staff had changed, grown stronger, and also attacked her. Apparently they had been afraid to do so before. She said that this had been one of the most "exquisite experiences" of her life. Many weeks later I heard that this woman was still appreciative of her experiences that evening. I was happy for us both: that she and I had learned so much about ourselves.

Assisting the Attacker

In some martial arts traditions, the teacher assists the student in overcoming him and in so doing helps to educate the attacker. The political implications of this are that a leader who is attacked is in a position not only to accept the attack and change but also to help the attacker create change in a useful way. In fact, the facilitator herself realizes that part of her job may be not only to resolve issues but also to assist others in processing the tensions of history in a more human fashion than in the past. Therefore, we should tell our attackers exactly what we think about their style. Were they too brutal, too shy, or too vague? Are their points well made? If not, then we should try to help them if we can.

The time of attack is an excellent moment to become a teacher of awareness. Being overcome may be profitable for both the attacker and the deposed leader if cooperative growth is your goal.

An Example from South Africa

I remember clearly my first trip to South Africa. I had a lot of optimism and excitement about testing my process work skills in South Africa. I did not realize that my optimism about group processing could be a response to their pessimism. I also did not know that their need to lead themselves out of their own situation was more important than my teaching them something about conflict resolution.

Live and learn! I learned the hard way that the members of any group are the only ones who can find resolution to their tension. The Africans must obviously be the ones to resolve their own tensions.

I said in the first meeting that the tools I was going to present were capable of solving the most difficult conflicts in several hours. I was unconscious about how my optimism and excitement polarized the group. A black social worker listened to my one-sided remarks and became my opponent who was going to prove me wrong.

She made a few negative comments in the beginning, but I overlooked them and launched into my work with the group. After a few hours, her pessimism naturally returned. She presented me with what she called an unsolvable conflict between two black groups in a Capetown township. I tried my best to solve the conflict. We went back and forth, switched roles, and did everything to counter her pessimism, until I realized that I was being attacked for being hopeful.

My antagonist stood up and admitted that she just wanted to prove that not all conflicts could be solved and that I could not be right. She awakened me in the last moment! She was not just pessimistic. I finally gave up my optimistic ways and agreed with her. I said not only that was I most likely incorrect but also that she was meant to be the leader and facilitator who could show the rest of us how to deal with the township tensions! Our conflict resolved on the spot.

That resolved the group for the moment. As everyone was silent, I realized many truths at once. People in conflict do not want to need help from outside to show them the way. Outside help has no grassroots effects. People living in conflict areas need love and encouragement first and education second. If a group in conflict does not get encouragement from the outside, the growing leaders within the group can only assert their potential power by inhibiting outside resolutions! The moral of this story is metaskills first, skills and information second.

Facilitation Exercises for Conflict and Attack

The following exercises are for those involved in public conflicts. They are meant as training exercises, not as a program to be followed during conflict. Hopefully these exercises will enable you to develop a generous view of others, allow you to tolerate and process violence, and increase your respect for the field in which we live.

1. Imagine the worst attack you have suffered as a leader in public.

2. Act out being the person who attacked you. Show someone else how to play this person and experiment with the following defense methods as they become real for you.

    a. *Admit that your attacker is correct* and that you need to change. Then do so.

    b. *Get behind the attacker's affect.* Find out what his or her hidden Ki or motivation is. Does he want to attack you? Does he want to make you realize that he is also an intelligent leader? Is he attacking you because he has been attacked and is in pain?

    c. *Take your own side.* Defend yourself and attack the attacker back. Or admit how hurt you are and show your hurt to the attacker.

    d. *Step out from your role* and help your opponent criticize you. If this is taking place in a group, ask others in the group to take your conflict as two timespirits meeting one another, as roles that everyone must fill.

    e. *Admit that your attacker is a teacher* and ask him to model the changes he expects you to be able to make in yourself.

f. *Complete the group process by noticing if everyone is involved* in the conflict you are having. Get the group to work on the issue themselves to discover how the conflict is valid or invalid for them personally.

g. *Work on yourself publicly.* Report to the attacker and to the group what is happening to you internally as you are being attacked. Attend to and complete all the experiences you are having inside until you find an inner resolution.

h. *Critique your attacker's methods of attacking.* Are they forceful enough? Are there double signals that make her incongruent? Is she sticking to her side even when she feels your own? Can she switch roles? Is she sufficiently compassionate? Use your awareness to take her side and help her grow! Do not just get bogged down in your abilities or inabilities.

i. *Ask for help.* Finally, ask her to help you grow. Were you honest about your feelings? Were you real and congruent? Were you also able to detach and flow with what was happening? And most importantly, does your attacker now trust you?

NOTES

1. Kisshomaru Ueshiba, *The Spirit of Aikido*, p. 23.
2. *Heiho Kaden Sho*, p. 23.
3. *Heiho Kaden Sho*, p. 23.
4. *Heiho Kaden Sho*, p. 23.

CHAPTER 6

Deep Democracy and
Innerwork

A ncient concepts of leadership included the qualities of priests, kings, queens, diviners, and politicians. For example, in the Chinese book of changes, the *I Ching*, the hexagrams frequently speak of the leader as a sage who looks toward heaven and attempts to convey this information to the people. The wise leader senses the present and the future timespirits and helps the people adjust to them.

The leader herself is a timespirit, a priestly role in a field; it is a role that no single individual should ever expect to fill sufficiently. Leadership is a group project, and all of us are necessary to fill it.

Expecting Attack

Nevertheless, we all tend to identify certain people with timespirits such as the leader role or the disturber role, and then we expect the people who fill the roles to be one-sidedly perfect or evil. A group cannot tolerate people in the leadership role who show anything but the archetypal qualities demanded of that role. We demand of our leaders that they be skilled politicians and diviners, powerful and loving at the same time. We demand nothing short of perfection from our leaders.

Thus, if you are called on to take a leadership role in a group, you should realize that that group will require you to be whole and fluid by representing the changing process of the public. Since the group's primary identity, the "we" of the group, is projected onto the leaders, as the field changes and evolves, the idea of the leader evolves as well, and the past identity for the leadership, or the "we" timespirit, will be challenged. Wise leaders will realize this and encourage their groups to develop their own evolving leadership potential.

Even the most capable leader must be challenged, because a group that is utterly satisfied with its leader would be one in which time had stopped. A good facilitator should even hope to be attacked, especially when working in groups other than her own; otherwise, the group would not have any leaders of its own.

For instance, I once worked with an organization that had been suffering from a "cold war." They had had so many conflicts over the past twenty years that they were close to disbanding. My wife, Amy, and I sat with the entire group one evening in order to help them process their tension. As soon as everyone had assembled, the members began screaming at each other. Every time we tried to say something or make a suggestion, the middle management leaders turned on us and blasted us. After just a few minutes, I felt miserable. I was hurt and hopeless and could not even follow what the people were saying.

I went off and sat in a corner by myself and worked on myself while the others continued to fight. It is not easy to work on yourself alone with so many people around, but I managed. I could not understand their attack on me, so I took over the side of the critics in my imagination. I said to myself, "Arny, shut up! We know what is right and how to do it." "I doubt that," I replied, "because if you knew what you were doing, you would know that violence is not going to help." That is just what I had failed to realize! I saw immediately that the people attacking me were potential leaders who were not doing their job very well.

Armed with this knowledge, I reentered the conflict and challenged my erstwhile attackers to show their true leadership. I challenged the most vocal critics, the middle management group, to model the kind of leadership they complained the executives lacked. Our critics now were able to do a marvelous job, in fact, and resolved the complex and long-standing problems. They solved their own problems and simultaneously demonstrated their immense leadership abilities.

Like all attackers, they were aware of the kinds of changes that needed to be made, but, also like all attackers, they were convinced that the big "bosses" needed to make these changes. When challenged and encouraged to make the changes, the attackers succeeded in solving their own problems.

Since the leader or facilitator represents a spirit in the organization, some issues a leader is attacked for may have little to do with her personal psychology. For example, if someone attacks the leader for being a tyrant, the leader should first examine herself for this problem, then ask if the tyrant is a background timespirit. She might help the group by embodying the tyrant and creating roles for a tyrant and a victim in the field. The leader should good-naturedly act like a tyrant and tell the others what to do. Embodying this role, or any role that the leader may be attacked for, is a step toward helping the whole group discover and transform its own viewpoints.

I remember once working with a schoolroom situation in which the learners were attacking the "teacher" for being a tyrant. Even when the teacher changed, the students continued their attack. At this point, I gave the tyrant a role in the group and told everyone to be quiet and settle down. Surprise! Everyone was happy. The tyrant had been insufficiently represented.

The Leader as Process Worker

Who is responsible for events in a group? The facilitator is usually given the responsibility, but she does not have sole responsibility for what happens. The entire field is responsible for the process that is happening. The leadership timespirit and everyone in the group are responsible for that process.

It seems, however, as if we place the responsibility for the world's events on our leaders and fail to realize that the course of events depends upon personal psychology, group awareness, and the global field. The best leaders can, at the most, be responsible for assisting a group in its awareness and for helping it process the evolving field and events.

The best leader may not be a leader in the conventional sense at all. A good leader is prepared to look at both her own personal psychology and the group's process as well in order to facilitate the group's process. She must take everything personally and at the same time not take everything personally. She must be able to give up her position and admit defeat and her faults, but she must also realize that she is unimportant and inconsequential to the entire development of the group. If she sees herself as too central to the organization, if she takes everything too personally, she robs the group of its own process and development.

Above all, a good facilitator realizes that the leadership position is just another role. It is a product, image, and feeling representing the group field, and it just happens to coincide, for the moment, with the facilitator's personal psychology. She understands that part of her momentary fate is to be a leader, just as other times her fate is to be a carpenter, parent, child, or disturber.

We either shy away from taking leadership because we expect ourselves to be perfect, or we are attracted to the role because of the power associated with it. Power, however, cannot ultimately be attached to the person in the leadership position; we confuse personal power with the field forces that create the leadership timespirit. A person in the leader role can only channel processes, not create them! Whenever we find ourselves scrambling to escape from the leadership role, we have identified too much with its one-sided nature.

The Leader's Unconsciousness

I learned long ago from private practice that fairness and neutrality to all parts of a group are essential leadership qualities. If I did not like something about a client, I would unwittingly try to repress my dislike. Of course, the client would sense this and eventually go elsewhere to complete his work. Now I know that disliking someone is a process that can be used constructively and usefully for the client. When I dislike something about someone, I am generally being disturbed by a part of that person that is not being used actively. If I can identify what disturbs me and then help the client have more access to that part and to use it more consciously in his interactions, my feelings change.

Objective neutrality is never completely possible. Our own psychology gets in the way and keeps us human. My first trip to the Middle East brought up my troubled relationship to my own Judaism, which I had not encountered before. I was born in 1940, at the beginning of World War II, and as a small child, I was beaten for being a Jew even before I was old enough to know what that was!

When I was four I wanted more than anything else to be an Italian Catholic like everyone around me and to grow up being as tough as the others. I managed to become a tough kid and avoided my Jewish complexes. I unconsciously became anti-Semitic, but it was not until I worked in Israel that this whole complex came out.

I had a feeling that our work in Israel would be troublesome, because even before I arrived, I was inundated with fantasies of conflict. I worked with my fantasies as much as I could, but a feeling of fear and trepidation still remained. I had recurring fantasies of being attacked and criticized, and I assumed that these critics and attackers in me had to be integrated. I tried to understand and integrate the attackers' energies and ideas as much as possible, but I failed to realize that the attacker in me was attacking me for being anti-Semitic!

My outer work in Israel went fairly well. The seminar participants were happy and interested in our work. However, in spite of myself, I lost my neutrality. I found myself harboring resentment and discontent toward the Israelis. I secretly judged and criticized them for their brutal repression of the Palestinians. I was at war myself, without realizing it, and I, too, had became a repressor, repressing and judging the Jews as I imagined they repressed the Arabs!

Sure enough, my anti-Semitism surfaced in the midst of a group process at the seminar when the theme of the Holocaust appeared, and I made the absurd recommendation that the group discover the Nazis in themselves by acting like Nazis. The intervention was well intended, but the metaskill—that is, the way I used the intervention—was unconsciously aggressive.

Even though the seminar participants were able to use the idea and even to make personal discoveries with it, my approach was unsuccessful because behind the intervention was a secret attempt to reeducate Israel. I was unconsciously getting them back for what they were doing to others. Even more disturbing, I was upset with them because I did not want to be identified with them.

I was lucky. The group of participants was probably the most liberal and enlightened in Israel at the time. They resolved the group process because of their own wisdom and because of the help of a wonderful and wise woman who stepped forward and pulled the group together. She spoke slowly and clearly, telling us that she, too, had once been full of hatred, fire, and rage about the past. But through her own innerwork and belief in herself, she had burned up the wood for that fire and finished up her own rage. She saved the day by filling the leadership role I was incapable of filling.

Grass-Roots Leaders

I learned many lessons from this. I now know that innerwork can never be finished. I remembered how essential detachment is. I saw how neutrality is disturbed by inflation, by believing that we know better. I thought I was wiser and knew better than the others. In the moment I believed that, I became just another timespirit in a troubled and conflicting group field. I also realized that I had repressed my own personal history and how important it is to realize our one-sidedness as well as our wholeness. If I do not admit that fate made me into being a man, a white person, an American, and a Jew, how can I also be a woman, a black person, a Christian, and a Moslem?

And finally, I learned that my own unconsciousness can be compensated for by others who are able to take responsibility for the leadership role. This realization has opened me up to the wisdom of others.

This experience resolved one of my most troubling questions. I have always been worried by the unconsciousness and ineptitude of world leaders. I have wondered how the world has continued to exist. How has the world managed to keep going, considering that there have been so few truly divine leaders? The experience in Israel showed me that humans have a divine aspect, a capacity for compassion and love and the ability, at the last moment, to fill the facilitator role. Without such spontaneous "grass-roots" leaders, this planet would have vanished long ago. Wherever such compassion occurs, we must honor it, learn from it, and praise the people who carry it.

Worldwork and Innerwork

I think of another example that illustrates the importance of being able to work on oneself in the midst of chaos. My wife, Amy, and I were working for an organization where we were living temporarily. Working for an organization and living on its property at the same time are a twenty-four-hour-a-day job, a job that requires a high degree of consciousness. It is similar to working in a foreign country at war. Living with the group with which you are working means that you cannot escape the field for a minute; you are inextricably tied up with all the timespirits and the field. There is nowhere to go to get outside the system.

One late evening at the organization, I was talking to one of the organization's managers, and, because of my fatigue, my one-sided criticisms and judgments of the organization slipped out. I acted like a wise guy and told the manager that I thought his group needed to change and be more sensitive. He nodded politely at my wise suggestions and seemed to understand my criticisms. Soon after we parted, however, I was visited by a number of others who were hurt and upset about the conversation I had had with the manager.

I had to wake up quickly and realize that there was no privacy. A field has no boundaries. Since my criticism had been thrown back in my face, I decided to accept my own ideas as applying to me. I worked on myself and tried to take on what I had accused the organization of. I assumed that I must be insensitive. Where was I being insensitive to myself or to others? Pursuing this question allowed me to make some important discoveries that relieved my negative feelings toward the organization.

Next time the entire organization met, I was able to be much more neutral and open. In fact, I found myself feeling loving toward the group. Before I could even speak about my feelings toward them, a small group of members came forward and insisted that we all proceed more sensitively.

Everyone in the room felt better! The people in that organization taught me how human it is to project upon a client, couple, or organization that only they need to change and to assume that the facilitator is in order.

Inside and Outside in South Africa

I suppose one of the strongest lessons I learned about innerwork and detachment happened during the end of my first trip to South Africa, just before the system of apartheid was seriously and successfully challenged. As I was leaving the country to go back to Zurich, I lost my temper and got into a terrible fight with the airline personnel.

The fight began at check-in. As I was waiting for my seat assignment at the airline counter, I just could not restrain myself anymore. I belligerently asked the woman at the counter, "How can you work in a place that discriminates so terribly against blacks?" To my surprise, she listened to my provocative remarks and quietly replied that she was thinking about leaving South Africa herself. She confided to me that the airline we were traveling on had a segregation policy "for white purposes." Blacks and whites were seated in different sections.

I had remained fairly calm during the whole trip, but now I felt completely justified in my anger. Even though I had seen much worse than this segregation during my stay, I lost my cool and became furious. I went with Amy and two other friends straight to the manager.

I confronted the manager about the segregation policy, and of course he exploded back at me. I ignored the recommendations of the wise Aikido masters and was in the midst of the worst kind of battle, yang against yang, power against power. The manager yelled at me, "Who told you that we segregated?" I wanted to protect the clerk at the check-in desk, so I yelled back, "You must have a segregation policy, or else you wouldn't be so upset." He threatened me with an investigation, and, seeing that the fight was going nowhere, I simply left.

Feeling dangerously self-satisfied (it is always dangerous to win), I boarded the plane, but my rage and indignation were still present. As soon as I got on the plane, I saw that the plane was indeed segregated. Whites sat in the front, followed by the Indians, and the blacks were in the back of the plane! I discovered that, to "punish" us, the manager had decided to seat us as the only whites in the black section!

I was so furious that I decided not to ride on that airline ever again. I was still in the field of South Africa, even as I was leaving it. Even as the airplane was taking off, I could not be contained. The devil had gotten in me, and I found myself breaking a cardinal rule of air travel: do not leave your seat during takeoff.

Still acting belligerently, I left my seat for the bathroom as we were leaving the runway. An enraged steward tried to restrain me, calling me names and forcibly restraining me. Suddenly, a fully intoxicated passenger stood up and tried to throw me back into my seat. I finally sat down, steaming but pleased that I had managed to give a good hard shove to the drunken passenger before sitting down. I was fuming, but I realized that it was time to work on myself.

This time I went inside myself and worked internally on the whole problem of segregation and discrimination. I sunk into inner space, working with my own internal biases, prejudices, repression, and victimization. I found out how I had been inhibiting myself in various ways and discovered that I had not been letting myself experiment with life the way I really wanted to.

I felt better, and after a few minutes, when we were in the air, I arose again to find that the field had changed. On my way to the bathroom, the drunken passenger whom I had elbowed earlier spontaneously came up to me and apologized for being so brutal with me! I was so shocked by his sudden humility that I could only mumble an apology for elbowing him. We became friends on the spot.

Inspired by this interaction, I went over to the steward who had been so nasty to me and apologized for having gotten out of my seat during takeoff. I gently recommended to him that we both keep our cool when serving others because we might avoid aggravating dangerous situations and better resolve emergencies. I told him I was learning about this myself. To my surprise, the man began to cry and said that he had never had anyone deal with him so sensitively before.

All of these experiences have shown me that people are not just good or evil but rather temporarily become timespirits, capable of changing when situations are processed. Innerwork is not the only response to outer injustice and to conflict. Confrontation and direct action are also necessary, but in situations where they do not work, or where they merely aggravate an already inflamed conflict, we have no choice but to work on the problem internally, to change the outer situation by changing the inner one. Working with a field means dealing with the issues wherever they appear: in groups, in our relationships, dreams, body symptoms, and fantasies. Racism, segregation, and insensitivity need to be worked with at all levels. In a relativistic universe governed by nonlocality patterns, process-oriented field work means following awareness, whether our focus is on outer or inner events.

Questions

1. What metaskills are talents of yours?
2. Which metaskills do you yet need to learn to deal with groups?
3. If one of your group projects has not gone well, what can you learn for your future work?

Exercises

1. Imagine your next potential group experience. What kind of person could possibly attack you?
2. Consider this attacker as an inner one and take his side until you can understand and feel the way he does about you.
3. Carry on an inner dialogue between the two of you until you become neutral, open to both sides or until the tension is gone.
4. Consider the possibility of talking about or replaying this attack and resolution scene at the next group meeting.

CHAPTER 7

The Taoist in Turbulence

The ability to do innerwork is not enough, for often we are forced to find the metaskills behind our capacity to work on ourselves in the midst of conflict. How do we gain access to our inner states in the midst of outer chaos and conflict? It is one thing to be a wise woman meditating on a mountaintop and another to have access to this wisdom in the midst of a gang fight, on a city street, or in a nasty argument. What models do we have for inner-centeredness in the midst of chaotic worldwork? Few, if any, of us have ever had teachers who could work on city streets and who could also be real, inward, effective, and heartful at the same time! Our high priestesses, gurus, and wise men are patterns for leaders, but many do not provide patterns for how to deal with street scenes.

The metaskills to have inner-centeredness, to self-reflect, and to balance in the midst of chaos and conflict are best illustrated with an example from physics. In this chapter, I will turn to fundamental principles in physics and psychology in search of greater depth and learning about chaos.

Awareness in Physics and Psychology

Process work, like physics, is a "bootstrap" theory. A *bootstrap theory* is a physicist's term for ideas that unify related theories of nature in such a way that even though the theories are not the same, they are mutually consistent with one another.

The bootstrap element of process work resides in its Taoistic basis. Process work has the potential to draw together modern disciplines such as the Jungian method of following the unconscious, the Gestalt focus on process, Carl Rogers's unconditional support for the individual, the transpersonal focus on the divine, and the systems principles in economics, politics, and physics. In a way, all of these are process psychologies, reflections of an ancient appreciation of the flow of life.

The bootstrap theory states that there may be no permanent constants in life. Albert Einstein and Werner Heisenberg were some of the first bootstrap theorists because their studies led them to the discomforting idea that physics no longer had permanent constants to fall back upon. Einstein, in particular, was upset about the fluidity of the ground of "reality," for its constant movement left him nothing firm on which to stand.

Process work, too, is based upon the assumption that experience is impermanent and nonabsolute. All states, experiences, figures, roles, and parts are timespirits. As soon as we work with our different experiences, be they in symptoms, dreams, relationships, emotions, movements, group atmospheres and processes, or even world events, they lose their constant quality. They change so dramatically that their original names are no longer valid. Even the patterns of turbulence and chaos, harmony and equilibrium are only momentary pictures of the flow that hold true for a moment and change the next.

Are there no constants in psychology? I believe there is one constant: awareness. As the physicists discovered, without the observer, there would be no physics. Everything that happens, happens in conjunction with the possibility that someone has become aware of it and observed it. In psychology, too, the only constant is the process of awareness, the observer who notices what happens and reacts to it.

Process work is the awareness of the moving ground, of the flow of events around and within us. Thus, according to this definition of process work, the basis of worldwork is awareness, not the states on which awareness focuses.

Awareness precedes our judgment of states of consciousness. Though we may distinguish "higher" from "lower" states of consciousness, kindness from brutality, good from bad, chaotic from normal, awareness shows that any given state is just a momentary experience with which we are identified.

Process work adheres to no personality theory because the entire focus is upon awareness. We almost never speak of the "ego," "self," "unconscious," or any other part as a constant, because process concepts are based upon apprehending and working with change, not with fixed structures. In this sense, it can be classified as a transpersonal psychology, since the idea of ego development is replaced with growth in awareness.

Likewise, process work cannot prescribe structures, states, or phases of growth for organizations, since the success of any group or business depends upon everyone's sensitivity and awareness. Of course, following processes means that prescriptions and states could, at given times, be necessary for an individual or organization!

The disadvantage to personality theories is that they are culture-specific and based upon social and cultural ideals. For example, Western psychopathology has an inherent standard of pragmatism associated with it. Many of the definitions of psychosis are based on the individual's state in relationship to functioning at work. The Western concept of ego is culture related; the ego is described in terms of the individual's adaptation to Western culture. By the same reasoning, certain concepts stemming from Eastern philosophies such as no-self or nonego are culture-specific. These concepts can easily slip into a prescriptive program for humility, introversion, and noncompetitiveness. Both the Western and Eastern personality concepts are valid and useful for the areas of the world where they were developed. They are specific to a culture, time, and location and therefore do not fit all people, places, and times.

Awareness, in contrast, is basic to modern, scientific, spiritual, and psychological traditions and so may well be a universal for psychology and for worldwork. In fact, as national boundaries become less important, and as communication between cultures becomes more available, awareness might gain in importance as a cross-cultural fundamental.

Awareness as a tool would help create a transcultural worldwork that would supplant the tendency of facilitators who diagnose, analyze, and prescribe solutions for people, with the assumption that organizations can be reprogrammed. Hopefully, the kind of worldwork I am describing will return a sense of deep democracy and will remain free from designations and judgments about good or bad personality characteristics, phases of development, neurosis and health, and consciousness and unconsciousness.

It is not possible to be entirely value-free and transcultural. Even in what I am prescribing here there are value judgments in my emphasis on Taoism and awareness. There are also times when lack of awareness, unconsciousness, and stupidity are necessary and correct. In fact, the *I Ching* supports all states, with good and evil, stasis and change—all are regarded simply as different states of being. Paradoxically, however, the *I Ching* also says that the person who follows the changes and the Tao is valued more highly than the person who tries to create the Tao. Likewise in process work, all states are seen as useful, yet the principle of awareness that observes and supports all the states is valued more highly than is trying to organize the states.

Being constantly aware is not the main goal; being unconscious can be fun and useful in certain moments. The awareness in process work is one that the individual is capable of using and awakening when necessary. The "sage" has to have the awareness of what is happening before he can have the chance to change or adapt to the spirit of the times.

Awareness and Change

The awareness of deep democracy could be the one constant in a universe that may have no other stable features. As a tool, this awareness allows us to value all states: love and anger, generosity and greed, arrogance and humility. In addition, awareness helps us value all states of development: resolutions are just moments in the midst of evolution. The attitude of awareness appreciates the need for resolutions, but by appreciating the other phases as well, relativizes the expectation and pressure to create a resolution. Attachment to peace will result in attempts to repress and control disorder, change, and disturbance. Such organization or control of processes is the only evil in the *I Ching*.

Should organizations be directed toward implementing new discoveries that arise from process work? When one is working with an individual, integration usually means that when something new happens, one is expected to integrate it and change according to the new self-discovery. Integration is an important part of psychotherapy, but awareness is even more important if we view not just the momentary discovery but also the entire lifetime of an individual or organization. All the breakthroughs, discoveries, parts of ourselves, emotions, and experiences are only of today and tomorrow. Awareness, however, is the power that gives us ongoing access to new states of consciousness and as yet unborn parts of ourselves and the world.

What is the role of awareness in organizations seeking change? Awareness might change behavior, but changing behavior does not always result in increased awareness or openness to other states. For instance, a company seeking financial prosperity will emphasize the need to resolve problems and make changes so that the whole organization works efficiently. How will awareness help a company fulfill its goal of increased productivity? Productivity and increased revenues are primary or momentary goals. They must be taken seriously, but the organization's level of awareness must also be investigated, for awareness is essential to reaching its goals.

Modern businesses and organizations realize today that if the people comprising the organization are not happy, then nothing works well. One of the best ways to make everyone happy is by including people in the organization, using each individual's awareness to help further the project. Our momentary problems need to be resolved, but the most satisfying and successful resolutions come from using awareness.

The following example illustrates how awareness can help a group diagnose and solve its problems. A business group was having trouble negotiating a contract between a new branch of the company and the mother organization. When the meeting of the two began, it became apparent that both groups were at a stalemate in the contract because there was a profound lack of trust between the members. In the course of the discussion, the members mentioned an individual who had stolen money from the organization. He had been one of the leaders of the parent organization, and it seemed clear to all that he was the reason for the mistrust. The contract was meant to protect the parties from possible thievery.

Instead of focusing further upon the details of the contract as a way to protect everyone from further theft, I suspected that the missing thief was part of the field, an important part that the others needed awareness of. I suggested to the group that we are all potential thieves: "Haven't you ever wanted to get more money for yourself?" I asked them playfully. I encouraged them to play the part of the missing thief.

The tense and difficult mood lifted as the timespirit of the thief emerged and transformed. One after another, each person took over the thief's role, confessing humorously desires for money, love, and more free time.

The group laughed at these confessions, and the tense field transformed into a partylike atmosphere! We may all be honest, hardworking citizens, but we are also potential thieves. Even though we work for an organization, we all want to get paid back for our labor. Playing the thief gave this group access to their neediness and greed, which ultimately brought the members closer together in friendship. Awareness helped create a contract by letting members drop the problem and create a community feeling instead. Once the background feeling of mistrust was aired, a spirit of community was created, and the members rapidly settled the contract dispute. This group's process is typical for most bargaining and negotiating processes. Negotiation happens most rapidly when the process in the background is lived.

Picking up the hidden Ki, the secondary processes of a group, is awesome and fun. It is a little like riding a horse backward. It means noticing and supporting things that others disregard or repress. For instance, requesting that a group of mistrustful and suspicious business people act out the thief seems at first a bit odd. To even make that intervention requires courage. Courage to notice and mention socially unpopular or forbidden behavior or emotions is a metaskill that one needs in order to use awareness of secondary processes.

Turbulence Patterns and Edges

Most group processes are relatively easy to follow. However, chaos and turbulence, disorder and disequilibrium are more difficult because they move so far from our consensus reality. Typical states of turbulence in psychology or in group processes are altered states, illness, insanity, and violence.

Turbulence and nonequilibrium situations are dealt with in modern physics within the context of chaos theory, by the growing science of wholeness.[1] This science sees all events as interconnected and stands opposed to reductionist approaches that attempt to understand events as the sum of causes and effects.

Turbulence adds a new dimension to the flow of events because we can no longer understand how the actions and behavior of one group are causally or temporally connected to those of another group. Suddenly we are dealing with events that seem random and haphazard. We are confronted with turbulent individuals, families, and groups. The following are examples of turbulence due to these factors in large groups.

1. **Increased speed and change.** A group, like a river, can change speeds rapidly. It can increase or decrease its growth due to political events, the death of central figures, or changes in the world situation.

For instance, Germany became possessed by Nazism while trying to find solutions to its economic problems. Recently, events in Eastern European communist countries have thrown those countries into an unprecedented rapid spurt of speed and change. The democratic movement, the urge for freedom, and the lessened restrictions are propelling them into turbulent situations.

2. **Individual disturbers.** Groups are sometimes thrown into turbulence and chaos when individual disturbers with new ideas appear. Sometimes disturbers are in strongly altered states of consciousness, displaying asocial, inappropriate, or dysfunctional behavior.

    For instance, a psychotic member of a family, an alcoholic or drug-addicted member of an organization, or an individual in the midst of an extreme state can throw an entire group into chaos.

3. **Repression and revolution.** Turbulence also arises when people who have been repressed suddenly overthrow their repressors or own inhibitions. Individuals and organizations undergoing such shifts in behavior no longer follow predictable patterns and expectations. There are many examples of this type of change in the sudden rise and fall of political leaders, rebellions of minority groups, leaders of businesses and organizations, and even families with teenagers.

    Any group that has dammed up certain processes will eventually and certainly enter into a turbulent phase when the dam is broken.

As a group or individual approaches issues and processes that have been disavowed, its predictable flow pattern becomes increasingly chaotic, illogical, and nonlinear. Irrational things, including illness, confusion, nightmares, fantasies, depression, synchronicities, or even parapsychological events, begin to happen.

However, the chaos of events at the edge is unpredictable only from the viewpoint of the original or primary identity. Thus illness seems chaotic and meaningless if we do not notice the many warning signals and symptoms beforehand. When we investigate illness, madness, or insanity, what at first appeared to be turbulence seems highly ordered, as I have shown in *City Shadows*.

Likewise, organizations that have repressed conflicts and processes in the background can be profoundly disturbed when harmony is thrown into chaos by the repressed elements. What seemed unpredictable and turbulent at first can always, upon reflection, be seen to have been knocking on the door long before it arrived.

The Eye of Turbulence

Thus conflict and chaos are predictable oscillations between two definitive patterns, and disorder is a matter of viewpoint. What seems improbable from the outside is predictable looking from the inside.

View A		View B
Events Understood from the outside		**Events Experienced from inside process**
Order	Disorder	New life
health	illness	new patterns to live by
sanity	madness	creativity
normal	altered states	being fluid
life	death	becoming yourself
marriage	divorce	ongoing relationships
peace	war	relationship processes
work-energy	entropy	awareness or unconsciousness

What at first seems turbulent or chaotic is, once given the chance to unfold itself, an exciting new pattern that has not been used until now. A new pattern appears in the midst of chaotic situations once we participate in them and unfold them. Facilitators need to know that there is a calm "eye in turbulence." This knowledge gives them the courage to allow small and large groups to temporarily enter into uncontrolled situations in order to find the new patterns that are trying to emerge.

Facilitators working with global and political situations need to know about processing chaos especially now, on the eve of a new millennium. Individuals, groups, and nations will need to go through rapid and unusual changes to meet the challenges of a planet in ecological and political crisis.

Our planet is already breaking out of known patterns and displaying chaotic behavior. Indigenous groups are disappearing. Economics is no longer a local process. The ecosystem is on the verge of collapse. Poverty and famine are on the increase. Crime, drugs, and addiction are rising.

New patterns are trying to emerge, but if we are not prepared for turbulent situations, these patterns will create pain and chaos instead of new lifestyles. Without appreciation for turbulence, we will merely try to regain control by reestablishing known and inefficient ways of doing things. If we are prepared, we have the philosophical and psychological framework necessary for creating "controlled abandon," letting things go and then picking up and supporting the emerging patterns.

In a recent class on street problems, we invited a group of about ten homeless, entirely drunk people into our class. Big Lion and Sharpshooter, as two men called themselves, seemed to be fighting over Sheila, while Tennessee and Alabama were yelling at the top of their lungs. Big Lion told us how furious his mother was at him for defecating in her backyard. General bedlam was breaking loose, and everyone was yelling and screaming at once. But Sharpshooter loved Big Lion's mother, who was apparently a very loving person. I saw that this "mother" who was full of love was trying to emerge, but any attempt to organize it by asking them to play it or talk about it failed. Suddenly, Big Lion began to sing, and everyone fell silent as love and compassion came through his voice, temporarily creating order out of chaos and "cleaning up" the situation.

Examples of numerous experiences in chaotic group situations come back to me. I have witnessed countless situations in which the group entered into a chaotic process, found the new, emerging parts of itself, and recreated a new center. I remember a group in Tel Aviv dancing furiously together after a fiery and chaotic conflict. I recall a group in Colorado Springs that found silence and peace after playing a war game in which they bombed themselves. And I remember a violent conflict between men and women in San Francisco that ended when everyone cried and suffered together.

New order can always be discovered in apparent chaos if we have the tolerance and patience to follow instead of programming nature, if we learn to live with the moving ground instead of pressing for solutions. If we look at history, we can see how nations and groups are constantly moving to the edge of new patterns, falling back, and then crashing forward into new identities.

I vividly remember the end of a long meditation seminar in Seattle. Each person was meditating on his or her awareness, mumbling quietly "I am aware of . . ." and filling in the empty spaces with feelings, visions, sounds, and so on. Suddenly the quiet murmuring was broken by the sound of a few people giggling. They stopped, and there was silence, but then the gigglers broke out again with more laughter.

Out of nowhere, it seemed, two roles emerged in our room. One was a teenage timespirit, and the other was the conservative parents or religious seekers who had no time for laughter.

The two timespirits laughed and yelled at each other, and a mock fight took place. Suddenly, someone's foot was stepped on. All of a sudden, our entire focus was upon the hurt foot, and everyone felt bad. "Hurt is present," one meditator observed, and all were quiet and intense, feeling the same pain.

This hurt generated the realization that under the surface was a turbulent conflict in which a lively repressed spirit was trying to emerge. But even beyond this conflict was an awareness of the pain we all suffer when conflict emerges unconsciously.

I suspect that tolerance for chaos may be the best preparation for the future. We are being challenged to assist these changes by observing, caring for, and tolerating nature. However, without awareness of all the parts that are present, chaos and turbulence may result not in new and useful patterns but in a recycling of history instead.

Questions

1. What fears if any do you have of group chaos? Experiment with the idea of becoming aware of and following human nature and the nature of the situation instead of trying to change it.

2. What order appeared in retrospect to be hidden behind apparently chaotic relationship or group scenes you have been in?

NOTE

1. Cf. Briggs and Peat, *Turbulent Mirror*.

PART III

GLOBAL WORK

CHAPTER 8

The Practice of Conflict Resolution

My wife, Amy, and I once worked with a couple in which the woman was suffering because her husband had fallen in love with another woman. We assisted them in processing their conflict.

The husband sat silently, and the woman said, "I feel depressed and rejected." We asked her to say more about her feelings, and, to our great surprise, she said that she actually understood her husband. He smiled, and she said that she loved him and wanted to support him in his need to grow and find out more about himself.

He remained silent while she was taking his side in the conflict. Therefore, we recommended to her to take his side even more congruently by standing next to him and speaking for him. She imagined her way into his feelings and, as if she were him, explained that he wanted to break out of his lifestyle, that his existence had become meaningless. He nodded in agreement, still saying nothing.

Suddenly the woman stopped and said that she no longer felt like supporting her husband. She said she felt detached and neutral. "So be neutral," we advised. "Be completely neutral. Step out and look at yourself and your husband." She left his side and stood up, looking at him and at where she had been sitting. She began to laugh and said she saw that she was supporting him more than she was supporting herself.

This insight provoked the woman to step back into the conflict, this time taking her own side. She said to her husband, quietly at first, but then with increasing vehemence, "Who cares what you are feeling? I hate you for neglecting me." She hesitated, turned to us, and said she felt more than she could say. We recommended that she use her whole body. She suddenly banged on the floor and screamed, "You lousy baby. I'm fed up with mothering you. What you need is a really strong reaction, and I'm going to give it to you!" She stood up and moved toward him, threatening him with her fist.

Suddenly the man spoke for the first time. He broke out in an enormous smile and said, "You are the gorgeous spontaneous woman I married. You're the person I've been looking for!" The woman yelled at him in a mixture of anger, fury, and delight. The mood had altered dramatically as their anger and fighting turned into love. They embraced each other, and Amy and I left the room. We had all had enough for the first round.

I have witnessed thousands of hours of conflict between individuals and organizations around the world, but the above story exemplifies several aspects of conflict resolution that I want to highlight in this chapter. First, the story shows that in some conflict situations, world-work procedures that require only one of the parties to have awareness are needed. Second, the crucial element in resolving conflict is people's awareness of their momentary state in the conflict. Are they on their own side, the other's side, or just neutral?

Finally, I want to show in this chapter that just about every person and organization goes through the same stages of development during conflict. In the type of conflict situations described here, I assume that the facilitator is not a neutral third party, as Amy and I were in the above-described situation, but is a member of one of the conflicting parties. Furthermore, I assume that this member has achieved a level of personal development recommended in the previous chapters.

The conflict resolution methods I describe are useful for long-standing conflicts in couples and groups of all types and cultures. They even apply to long-standing conflict in which one or more of the parties refuses to negotiate with the other party. (Frequently, one member of a dispute refuses to sit down at the table with the other party. Most negotiating and conflict resolution procedures require all participants in the conflict to be present.)

After studying some of the typical conflict resolution sessions I have experienced in many parts of the world, I have been able to outline several stages of conflict resolution. First, I will describe these and ways of working through them. I plan to encourage anyone involved in a conflict to work with it. A disadvantage to writing out stages of conflict resolution is that they may be taken as a program for doing conflict resolution. I hope that the reader sees these stages as guidelines meant to increase awareness in conflict, not as rules to apply mechanically.

The central, guiding awareness question in conflict is, "What am I feeling and doing, and in which stage of conflict am I?" All the interventions that I recommend are derived from momentary feelings and the stage of conflict. Use and develop the following recommendations to awaken your awareness and to discover the stages you and your partners are in.

The idea is to practice using your awareness in a conflict situation with the help of the following material in order to enter the conflict, help complete the stage it is in, and move it toward resolution.

Though the interventions in this chapter have been found to temporarily resolve even long-time conflicts in groups, there are a few limitations to their efficacy.

1. **Awareness.** For a group to resolve its conflict, there must be a few people in a hundred who are trained in these conflict resolution procedures. These people must be able to maintain some degree of objectivity, be able to work on themselves rapidly in public, and be aware of the field concepts of the work.

2. **Personal development.** The facilitators must be capable of deep democracy—of remembering and supporting all sides of the conflict, even when they are one of the parties involved. This means that the metaskills described in previous chapters must be as present in conflict as the skills I describe here.

3. **Time.** The conflict resolution procedure presented here will help to resolve even violent conflicts within several hours. However, resolution is a process, only one state in an evolution. Creating useful experiences from long-standing tensions cannot be done in the large group alone; it requires resolution and work at many levels, including working with individuals and small subgroups of the larger group.

4. **Self-help.** Complete resolution means that the group has changed and developed the ability to work with its own conflict. It can take months for a large group to reach a stage of completion in which its own natural leaders step out of their own troubles and begin to learn methods of conflict resolution.

Conflict Resolution Stages

1. Avoiding vs. Understanding

The first stage of conflict resolution is to do what most of us do when confronted with conflict: avoid it. Forget the conflict. Try to ignore it and act peaceful. If that does not work, and it usually does not, the following ideas may help get you over your desire to avoid conflict.

Self-Discovery   You are not alone in wanting to avoid conflict. Most of us tend to avoid it. However, the potential for growth and self-discovery lies in conflict. That conflict is a chance to get to know the previously undiscovered sides of yourself. It may help your fear of and discomfort about conflict change to excitement about personal growth.

Conflict Is Normal   Everyone experiences inner and outer conflict at one time or another. It is a normal occurrence, a sign of your tendency toward self-balance and of development and growth.

Conflict Is Multileveled   Conflict is not only an expression of your own troubles, complexes, or personal psychology. Conflict is also a combination of your own internal tensions, your relationship troubles, and group and world problems. In the case mentioned above, the woman's conflict involved her own personal development and relationship but also the current development and change of men and women around the world.

Conflict Can Create Community   In the above example, the couple itself was awakening and changing. When we work on conflict in groups, a useful attitude is that a group needs conflict in order to understand itself. Conflict may be the field's way of getting to know and appreciate its parts and of realizing its full self.

Perhaps you will find the courage to enter conflict if you understand that your personal role in the conflict is really that of a time-spirit in the global field. Regardless of what the nature of your role may be, filling it consciously is a means of helping the field know itself.

2. Noticing

After first trying to avoid the conflict, the next stage of conflict work is to notice the conflict. Sometimes conflict is not easily noticeable; sometimes it is not overt. The following are some typical signs and signals of conflict:

verbal disagreement

lack of overt communication

remaining separated by space or time

gossiping about the opponent

having bad dreams or fantasies about the opponent

being suspicious or mistrustful of the opponent

3. Determining Malignancy

Some conflicts are minor, others severe. Conflicts like that of the man and woman described above, which threaten to destroy one's home life, business, family, and so on, are malignant conflicts.

If you notice conflict, when will you work on it? Why work on every conflict? If a conflict is malignant, it should get our full attention. Whether or not a conflict is malignant is an individual matter; it need not be agreed upon by consensus. Here are some of my ideas of what makes a conflict malignant and in need of work:

The problem is festering, producing bad feelings, and increasing over time.

People have been gossiping for a long time. The gossip is malevolent and includes an increasing number of people.

The problem never resolves itself and ruins the atmosphere to the point that people try to stay away.

You avoid the problem because of hopelessness or lack of courage.

More and more people are involved in the conflict.

4. Making a Conscious Choice to Get Involved

If you are going to try to resolve the conflict, then you should prepare yourself. The moment to enter a conflict is the one you choose. People who enter conflicts without preparation may do well, but those who make conscious decisions about entering a malignant conflict inevitably are more successful and gain more from the experience. Furthermore, if others are involved, never press them to be present. They, too, need time to prepare.

Awareness and Courage   The best preparation is awareness. Awareness may be more important than courage in conflict work. Courage makes you feel strong and thus tempts you to win and overpower others even when you are afraid. Improving awareness of your feelings detaches you from the pressure of winning and losing and gives you a more generous and stable attitude from which to work.

Fear   If you are afraid, try to determine why. Are you afraid because the unknown excites you, or are you afraid of losing? Fear polarizes you into being weak or strong. Check out your motives. If you want to become aware, strength and weakness become irrelevant.

If you continue to be afraid, find out what you are afraid of. If you are afraid of your opponent, ask yourself whether you are afraid of your own anger or power as well. We frequently fear others' violence and rage because our own power is inaccessible to us. Some fears are due to our unknown powers.

In conflict resolution seminars that we have given, the following exercise has been useful for those preparing for a conflict. Imagine a conflict you wish to clear up. Think about the conflict and ask yourself the following questions:

> What is your reason for not entering this conflict? If you are afraid, imagine what or whom you are afraid of and experiment with being this thing or person.

> Is your fear due to loss of awareness during fights? Do you become unconscious, dizzy, or moody? What mood specifically do you need to be more aware of? How can you remember this mood and use it better?

5. Addressing the Conflict Partner

If you have noticed and prepared yourself for entering a malignant conflict, you may now find yourself ready to address the problem. Ask yourself whether you are ready.

Set It Up   If you are ready to enter the conflict, set it up. Do not just jump in, but rather try creating a ceremony, a conflict ritual.

Remember the martial arts attitude of exactitude and awareness. Set up a time and place on which both parties agree. If you simply start in right away without consulting your opponent, the two of you will end up fighting about the resolution methods and never get to the issue. If your opponent will not appear, then you can work on the problem internally. Remember, conflict is a field phenomenon, and only the times can indicate when to deal with the tension internally, in relationship, or in a group process. In any case, let us imagine your partner is ready to come to the table.

You may want to make a note of the following steps and use them when you need them. You can even share this with your opponent, since there are no secret strategies in this work; the goal is awareness, not winning.

Address the Problem When you address the problem, state your motivations for trying to resolve the conflict. You could even mention that you hope for peace or that you are disturbed by the coalitions and groups forming around the two of you. This is the time to speak about your goals and motivations for working out the conflict.

Ask your opponent if she would be willing to address the problem. Do not just raise the conflict issue but ask if she agrees to work on it. If she refuses to do so, ask her if she has an idea how to resolve the conflict. If her solution is not useful to you, ask her if she would consider the help of a facilitator or outside agency. If she refuses all your approaches, then take the conflict internally and try to solve it there. Again, not everything must be worked out directly; some problems are matters for inner timespirits.

6. Processing Awareness

Let us assume that you and your partner are ready to proceed in your conflict resolution. The next step is to develop your awareness of where you are in the conflict process. A conflict has several states. Are you neutral, on the other person's side, or on your own side?

These questions are for you alone, not for your opponent. Only require yourself to be aware; do not require that your opponent change or become aware. Insisting that your opponent change or do something might be an inflated and unrealistic supposition.

Like the woman in the example above, many people find themselves siding with the opponent. If you are feeling protective of your partner, regardless of your reasons, then be protective. Do not worry about your motivations here. You might find yourself supporting the opponent because you are afraid of losing her friendship. Support her congruently.

Perhaps you are in a neutral position. Do you feel apathy, coolness, indifference? Perhaps you are really very detached about the conflict. Go ahead and express your neutrality.

Perhaps your awareness tells you that you are possessed by your own side. If this is the case, then you should begin by stating your own side.

7. Taking Your Own Side

Many skip this stage of conflict and immediately take the other person's side or express their neutrality. However, at one point, regardless of what else is happening, you will find yourself needing to take your own side.

Know Your Feelings   Many of us need to learn how to know what we are feeling. State your feelings directly. Be exact about your emotional experience. If you are upset, be upset. Do not hide it. Show it, express it, and then let go of it when it is finished. Be as real as possible about your needs, pain, fear, anger, hurt, or jealousy.

If your partner is afraid of emotions, then try expressing them in other channels. This means that rather than moving or yelling if you are angry, express your anger or hurt in a picture, for example. Try reporting to your opponent about your state using images.

Remember the Timespirits   It is helpful to remember the field; what you feel may be a part of our whole world. It may be a role, a timespirit in a field that is not sufficiently expressed; in such a case you are doing something for everyone.

Work on Your Altered States   Perhaps you have been avoiding taking your own side because you are afraid of your own rage, hurt, disappointment, or love. These procedures will not work unless you also study the feeling states that you tend to repress.

Take a moment and consider which feelings come over you in a conflict: fear, anger, hurt, sadness, and so on. Try feeling those emotions and expressing them to yourself. Discover them and the edges you have to them. Try to accept these states.

It is important to find out about the edges you have against these emotions. Which emotions can you express? With which do you not want to identify? If you do not like some of your states, it is important to admit it. If you try to inhibit some of your emotions, or if you try to hide your dislike of them, your partner will notice and attack you for lying or being dishonest.

Taking your side can have many forms. One way of taking your side is to report on the inner experiences you are having. If your emotions are not clear, then you should work on yourself in front of your opponent. Ask yourself out loud what you notice, what feelings, images, and experiences are happening in you. Then follow these experiences and report on them as they arise.[1]

8. Deescalating to Neutrality

Notice Your Feelings of Discomfort   After you have taken your side and expressed your feelings completely and honestly, you will probably begin to feel uncomfortable in your position, maybe because you feel sorry for your partner, maybe because you sense that you are being too one-sided, or maybe because you notice that you no longer fully agree with yourself.

Some people feel uncomfortable just having strong emotions in the first place. Cultural norms repress emotion, particularly conflict, and make us feel guilty for broaching the subject. If you feel guilty for having brought up the conflict, do not press yourself to go further. Withdraw.

Notice Your Own Deescalating Signals and Follow Them   Let yourself change. Once you take your own side, chances are you will begin to deescalate. Deescalating signals are those signals of withdrawal, such as quieting voice, moving away, looking away, or simply losing interest. If you find yourself moving away physically, then do it with awareness. Do not continue to act angry or hurt if you are not. Once you have taken your side, watch your tendency to stay attached to anger and hurt. If you are attached to these feelings, then go ahead and take your side, but then let go and step back to the neutral position.

When people get stuck in their viewpoints, it is usually because they either have not completely expressed them or have become attached to and identified with them and have lost awareness of their deescalating signals.

9. Being Neutral by Nature

Some people will find themselves in the neutral position. There are many reasons for being in the neutral and detached position. Some people are neutral by nature. Often you find yourself feeling detached because you have burned up the emotions that were typical of you before. When you find yourself feeling detached, step out and admit it; otherwise, your partner will notice and accuse you of being aloof.

Neutrality is still a position within the relationship field. If you become neutral, then step away from your position. Literally step away physically so that you do not identify with the space or feeling you were occupying before. Look at yourself and your opponent from the neutral position. Remember the woman in the example earlier? After she had taken her husband's side, she looked at herself and saw what needed to come next. So step out of your role, take a good look at your partner and yourself, and give a report of how you and your partner look.

As you step outside, try to have a look at yourself in your previous position. Describe yourself to your partner. Tell your partner how you see yourself now, what you see from the outside. Perhaps you become aware of yourself, of how you are trying to grow, of what you are attempting to do in the relationship. Communicate this to your partner. Try to give her a picture of where you are now, as if looking down from a mountain peak.

Risk looking at your partner as well. Perhaps you have a recommendation for her. Do you think she could do something to get her point across better? Would you like to help her in some way? If you feel she needs help, then this is the moment to leave your neutral detachment and to get back in the conflict. This time, however, take her side.

10. Taking Your Partner's Position

Taking the opponent's side will work as a conflict resolution procedure only if it is genuine. Many of us take the other person's side when we do not genuinely feel it. Either we are conforming and adapting too quickly, or we are acting benevolent and superior. If you cannot take your partner's side congruently, then try to determine whether you are still on your own side or if you are feeling neutral.

Have Compassion   Perhaps you are feeling compassionate toward your opponent. If this is occurring, not out of a sense of duty but as something genuine, step out of your side and ask if you can be of help. Use your compassion to help your opponent express his position better.

Read the Signals   Taking the other's side means more than just being compassionate. Observe your opponent. Look at how he stands, how he looks at you, and try to imagine the feelings he is having. Help him to express them.

Do not use this opportunity to mimic your opponent. Do not provoke him but use your awareness and your compassion to discover and feel who he is. If you find yourself provoking or mimicking him, then provoke directly; don't mimic.

Check the Feedback   The measure of how well you are doing is your opponent's feedback. You have successfully read into your opponent's signals if she sits back and relaxes or is touched by and thankful for what you are doing. However, misreading your opponent's signals can also turn into something useful. If you are wrong about what you imagine your opponent to be feeling or thinking, then you should ask her to correct you.

There are important psychological reasons for taking your partner's side. We come into conflict with others because of parts of ourselves that we, like the opponent, are unconsciously upset about. After all, we would not be in a conflict if a part of ourselves did not agree with the opponent.

11. Cycling

After having used your awareness to take your own side, your partner's side, and the side of neutrality, the conflict either ceases or cycles and enters a new level. Perhaps you or your opponent apologizes for having been hurtful. New issues, new reactions, or new feelings come up. At this stage of the conflict, the work continues as before. Use your awareness, go inside, and find out what your feelings are and what side of the conflict you are on. If you do not know your feelings or feel unconscious or incongruent, step into the neutral position. Take a good look at yourself from outside and advise yourself from the neutral position.

Lack of Expression   The conflict may be incomplete because you did not fully express the feelings on your side, or perhaps did not completely understand your partner's position.

12. Leaving the Field

Retreating   If you have adequately found out which side you were on, expressed that side, and followed all the changes, you may find both yourself and your opponent automatically retreating. This is a subtle moment to notice. Use your awareness to see if there is a slight moment of relaxation, a flicker of a smile, a small sigh of relief. If so, let go and leave the field.

This is an extremely important moment in a conflict. It is easy to miss signals of deescalation because most people avoid conflict for so long that when they finally enter it, they become addicted to the state and resist leaving it behind. Notice your deescalation signals and then forgive your opponent and yourself as well.

Learning   Perhaps both you and your opponent are excited by something you have learned. If so, try to identify what you learned about your partner or yourself. Is this a situation where you can share what you have learned about yourself?

Your Opponent Wanting the Chance to Experience Your Side Your opponent may want to learn more about you. Until now we have assumed that you are the only one interested in conflict resolution, because requesting that both people be willing to work on the conflict would have placed an unnecessary restriction on the work at an early stage. Yet your opponent might want a chance to find out more about you and about the conflict. This could be the moment when real sharing can begin.

Becoming a Teacher   Sometimes your partner may even want to learn from you about conflict resolution. Now is the moment for you to stop being an ordinary participant in a conflict and to share your knowledge of conflict facilitation.

13. Working in a Group

The simplest situation is one in which the sides of the conflict dissolve, and all is well. A common situation is when friends or neighbors continue to discuss the conflict even after the two sides have completed their personal work. This means that the timespirits are still around, not that the two conflicting positions have more work to do. The conflict is now a community or field issue asking to be addressed through group-work. This is the moment for setting up roles and asking the group members to fill them until the conflict is resolved in the community.

14. Working Individually

If conflict resolution between warring parties in the large group-work does not create resolution, then the problem may be approached through individual work. Everyone concerned must consider the conflicting sides as two inner parts of themselves that are asking for an individual resolution. This would be the moment to change levels in the group process and to invite everyone to work individually to find personal answers to collective problems.

Summary

1. Process conflicts when they arise. Do not wait until they become unnecessarily polarized.

2. If you avoid conflict because you are hopeless or afraid, remedy this by training yourself in conflict work.

3. Use your awareness to find out which position you are in: on your own side, on your opponent's side, or in a neutral position.

4. If you get stuck on your side, you may not have been able to complete the real feelings you have, or you have been hurt by the other person and cannot express your hurt and anger.

5. If you feel neutral, do not merely stay in that position to avoid the conflict or to act superior and detached. Use your neutrality to help both yourself and your opponent by observing the conflict from the outside and making recommendations.

6. The things that your opponent accuses you of are, even to a minor extent, your own double signals, feelings, and emotions that you have or have had. Do not forget that your opponent is also a part of you that is upset about something in you.

7. No one wins a conflict unless both feel understood and enlightened about the theme or the nature of the other. Enlightenment is a field experience; unless all feel enlightened, no one feels enlightened.

Conflict Resolution Exercise

1. Choose a friend to help you with the exercise.

2. Describe a real conflict with a real opponent you have in your life right now.

3. Have your friend play the opponent.

4. Take your own side strongly.

5. Notice when you are uncomfortable with your position and either become neutral or take your opponent's side.

6. Go back to your original role and notice if things have changed or continue until the conflict disappears or until both sides feel they have won.

7. Add new methods and steps to the work and write me about it.

NOTES

1. See Mindell, *Working on Yourself Alone,* for a description of innerwork methods in relationship conflict.

CHAPTER 9

Minority Awareness

The next century will inherit central, unsolved problems: the repression of people due to ethnic, racial, religious, social, economic, or gender factors. Though I am horrified by the treatment of minority groups around the world, I am also excited by their potential power. The minority position contains nothing less than the key to the future. And individuals who disturb the ruling powers by representing different ideas and lifestyles have an important opportunity to raise our global consciousness. This chapter describes the development and training that we may use to support the minority viewpoint for our own, our group's, and the world's good.

The Denial of Minority Issues

Many of us may not realize how we unconsciously repress others. Even psychotherapeutic and spiritual groups that do not directly intervene in social issues are implicitly prejudiced, or even racist and sexist. Today, it is not enough for a group or government to say that it is open to everyone, for many implicit economic or social pressures prevent many from total participation. Therapeutic communities in particular are racist and sexist if they focus solely upon inner or individual issues, because only those with enough money to eat can afford to devote a lot of time to themselves and their intimate relationships.

Inner-directedness alone can be racist, antisocial, and discriminatory. Spiritual traditions and therapies of the future must intervene in public life if they are to create viable and sustainable futures. They must assist their practitioners to understand and process repressive assumptions such as the belief that gays and lesbians are neurotic. Otherwise, we will have to understand innerwork as the privilege of those in the upper middle economic classes who are either heterosexual or able to repress their true natures.

Thus, lack of interest in minority issues is one way the majority represses groups who have little political power. A second way is expecting individuals from these groups to quickly recover from their sadness and anger about oppression. Why do we have so little tolerance for the pain of an oppressed person? We all remember how painful it was for us to be hurt as children by adults and how long we were angry and depressed about this. Why, then, do we have so little tolerance for those from oppressed groups who are crying in pain from decades or centuries of abuse?

It is repressive to expect an abused minority to take back negative "projections" and remain quiet simply because the majority cannot stand the noise. The minority individual suffers not only because of past abuse but also because of the present intolerance to his or her suffering. For example, the pain caused by the white community to the black community, the unfulfilled American constitutional promise of civil rights, the present global battering of gays and lesbians, the way in which women are consistently downed, and the unrealistic heroic expectations societies require of men should remind us that anger in our environment is not coming solely from our inner life. Nor are persistent self-criticism and feelings of inferiority signs of merely personal neurosis in a minority member.

Oppressed individuals and groups are in a difficult position. Their very being represents a viewpoint, issue, or opinion that runs counter to that of the majority or collective. There are very few options for minorities. They can do as they are asked, repress their natures and viewpoints, and adapt to the collective view or revolt. Peacefully working for change by reeducating the majority is possible only for those fortunate enough to look in from the outside or for those lucky few who have arrived at a state of detachment in the midst of their pain.

All around the world, individuals and groups are polarized into majority and minority conflicts, even though there is a strong tendency to deny and ignore the existence of repression. Yanoov[1] reports that the residents of a small Israeli town in 1985 identified the following opposing groups in their community:

Conflicting Groups in an Israeli Town

Males	Females
Young people	Adults
Poor	Rich
Conservatives	Liberals
Working class	Intellectuals and scholars
Criminals	Honest citizens
Fundamentalists	Secular groups
Ashkenazim (Western Jews)	Sephardim (Eastern Jews)
Native Israeli	Recent immigrants (Ethiopians)
Hawks	Doves
Members of the coalition	Members of the opposition

Yet not one person in the village mentioned to the interviewers the existence of Arab-Jewish conflict! The denial of this core minority problem is characteristic of the entire world. Central minority issues are repressed, denied, and ignored by all of us, not just by repressive governments. I have heard blacks and whites alike in South Africa deny that there was a black-white problem. How often do Californians discuss discrimination against Hispanic or Asian immigrants? Few residents of a middle-class New England town will admit to their reactions against black families moving into their neighborhoods. The Swiss neutrality is betrayed by their sometimes overt discrimination against Italian workers and the rising number of neo-Nazi groups in their country. Nor do Japanese citizens mention discriminatory policies toward foreigners in their country. In just about every group in the world at this time some form of discrimination against women and homosexuals exists.

Minority Members and Extreme Group States

When an individual speaks up in a group, representing an unpopular or minority view,[2] the situation can quickly heat up, escalating into a violent and chaotic extreme state. When an organization or group begins to look at disavowed, repressed, or otherwise unconscious secondary processes, or when someone speaks from a minority position, the primary focus and goals of the group are upset. Thus, disempowered minority groups or individuals are often seen as disturbers by the people in power.

Yet a city or country that violently represses a part of itself, as in the Chinese government's repression of the students' democratic revolt in 1989, is on a self-destructive course. The law of self-balancing shows that opposites eventually balance. A violent act in one direction will eventually be countered with a violent act in the other direction.

It is impossible to fully repress a minority position, since it is a timespirit. An individual or subgroup that voices its dissent in a group or organization can be killed, but their message continues unrepressed. Even if the minority is thrown out or forced to submit, a timespirit cannot be killed. It uses numerous tactics to thwart the primary focus of the group. A minority may appear to comply, but the group spirit and atmosphere of even a large organization will eventually be ruined by the mood of resentment, mistrust, and hatred.

Being repressed is such a severe and painful experience that many minority uprisings happen spontaneously and with such power that little or no awareness may be present. The desire to seek revenge and inflict the hurt that one has been suffering is a universal experience in minority "hot spots" around the globe. The unfortunate result of the conflict between minority group members and the majority is that minority members are usually unwilling or unable to help both themselves and the whole. Thus, disempowered groups often mirror those in power: both consider only their own view. Therefore, it is all the more important to note exceptions to this tendency, such as the U.S. civil rights movement of the 1960s.

The Lack of a Metacommunicator

The typical structure of a minority-majority conflict is that there is no *metacommunicator*, no neutral witness to the conflict. Revolution almost always has only two parts, the repressed and the oppressor, the alternative and the mainstream. The third part, the metacommunicator, who stands outside the turbulent storm, is missing.

Neither side feels able to occupy the metacommunicator position of neutrality or fairness because, regardless of the issues, everyone identifies only with their feelings of hurt, anger, and victimization. All are simply too depressed or furious to notice detachment or the other's side. The minority conflict flips the field into a turbulent and chaotic state, while the world outside stands by intolerantly, thinking that both sides in the conflict are crazy.

The outside world looking in becomes, for better or worse, a failure at metacommunication. It judges, diagnoses, and treats one side or the other in the conflict as subhuman. A group or country in revolution is punished and diagnosed by the rest of the world in the same way that doctors, family members, and colleagues act toward someone going through a psychotic episode.

The aloof and superior outside world is often as unconscious about its position as the members of the battle are about theirs. All are possessed by their own states. The outside world fails to see its position as a role in the conflict. Thus, there are no local battles. Every local battle is a world war in which everyone is a part.

Minority Awareness

It seems almost miraculous that in the midst of this chaos, semi-illuminated leaders arise to set new examples of solving problems. Martin Luther King and Mahatma Ghandi are examples of those who tried to awaken the disempowered to their potential strength and capacity to move beyond prevailing government powers. Today there are many in peace and environmental movements doing similarly.

The first step for those of us who are interested in creating change is realizing that the issues of the conflict get more attention than the way we process the conflict. There are many different minority situations in every place on earth: blacks and whites, men and women, Third World and industrialized nations, homosexuals and heterosexuals, insiders and outsiders, rich and poor, and so on. Our attempts to resolve these issues betray our need for more training in conflict resolution. We frequently become possessed by one role or timespirit and forget our other sides. We contribute to polarizing the world into turbulence by insisting on only our own view, instead of trying to attain an overview that would allow us to create the lasting changes we need.

We should remember that there are two types of status quo. One is the oppressive manner in which the ruling power maintains life the way it is. The second is the bloody way in which history has often proceeded, where one group eventually overthrows the other. A real change would be developing a new method of transformation.

The Psychology of the Minority Position

Those in the minority position usually know that they are in the minority. However, sometimes we need to remember that when we are in a minority position, irritation becomes frustration and turns to discomfort, then rage, and finally even righteousness and inflation. The altered states of consciousness we go through as a minority member cause us to lose the overview of our situation.

The minority-majority split is basic to all fields; only the issues and language change from situation to situation. There are a primary group identity and a secondary, disavowed identity in every group process. This split is always characterized by tension, segregation, anger, and hate. It is inevitable for individuals and groups to create minorities by creating an identity that demarcates an accepted from a rejected form of behavior. Every group has an identity that states, "We are this and not that!"

The following characteristics are typical minority position experiences.

1. You know you are in a minority position if you feel judged, persecuted, misunderstood, or undervalued.

2. Your minority position is usually complicated by the fact that you feel unsupported not only by the majority but also by your own group. You may not find support for your ideas even in your own group.

3. You feel persecuted and, given the chance, would persecute the majority. Thus, the concept of victim is usually not an accurate description of your position. Your frustration makes you sometimes resemble your opponent.

4. You are like the majority in the way you treat yourself. You persecute and victimize yourself with self-doubts. You may even secretly doubt your own group and its ideas.

5. You feel patronized by the majority. You are often denied adult privileges and dealt with like an untouchable person, a child, or an insane person. When it comes to stating your own viewpoint, you may even find that for some reason you will not or cannot voice your opinion in a coherent manner.

6. You sometimes have trouble formulating things clearly enough to be understood. You often become depressed by your inability to speak up, thinking that it is your own fault. Since the kinds of

things that bother you may be inappreciable or imperceptible to others, you sometimes feel a bit crazy.

7. You are afraid to speak, because if you do, you could be arrested, hurt, lose your job, or die.

8. You sometimes feel wiser than others or like the fool or outsider who sees what others cannot see, because, in fact, you are the wise one, fool, and outsider. The wise one, fool, and outsider are repressed roles in most groups. They need to be represented. Stand for this position, represent it because the field needs it.

9. You feel confused, restless, and paranoid. You cannot pay attention, and you feel the leadership or government is after you.

10. You need help but cannot admit it. Therefore, you seek coalitions with people outside the situation. You feel weak about dealing with the field as it is. You should seek coalitions consciously. Get the help you need.

Encouragement

Unfortunately, there is no training for being a member of a minority or disempowered group. You are in new territory. You should consider that the field in which you live needs you to find out more about itself, that the collective is asking you to help it express itself. By being the channel for their opinion or position, you will help everyone.

Your minority position expresses the suffering in the whole field, and you should understand that many will not be able to listen. Your position is a disturbing one for others. Yet, if you were able to find some reserve and insight, you could help everyone. However, if you become identified with your minority position, the chances of your being badly hurt increase. Make a conscious choice whether to do nothing and remain hopeless, to maintain your reserve, or to become enraged.

Being a hero or heroine can be meaningful for others, but it can also mean that you will be injured. You need to carefully consider whether dying, losing your job, being jailed, or being hurt is what you need. There is a time for everything: for waiting, for facilitating, and for becoming a charismatic heroine.

The tense fields of conflict may produce fantasies of death in you. If it is time to detach from the outer conflict and proceed with facilitation work, then consider your death fantasies further on an inner level. Try to metaphorically "kill yourself" and no longer identify with your person. Now you may become something different than a normal participant in the conflict. You are no longer a victim, hero, or murderer but an objective, fair witness who is free to do anything, including awakening others. Your ability to do this may depend upon the spirit of the times as well as your proficiency at innerwork.

If you find yourself in this detached position, you will be able to maintain your reserve and work for everyone. The following recommendations may now be useful for you.

1. Know Thy Monster

Most groups behave pleasantly when all goes well. However, even the nicest, most civil, generous group, when disturbed, will become a belligerent monster. This is one reason why we are afraid to speak up in public. Therefore, one of the most important tasks is to study and observe the group's identity, its primary process. Only by having studied the group carefully will you be prepared to deal with the monster when it awakens.

2. Feed the Monster

Learn to feed the monster. Feeding the monster means being able to satisfy and pacify it so that you are not eaten alive and so that it is open to the possibility of change. If you do not feed the group monster, it reacts like a trapped and panicked animal. It feels endangered; it senses approaching death and will react violently.

If you want to awaken others, your first job is to set the stage for interaction by recognizing the nature of the majority and realizing that both its position and your own are timespirits that will change with and without you! If you want to find out what type of group you are in, disturb it a little and find out what type of monster is present. The first step is to analyze what type of group primary process you are in conflict with. The following are possible group identities.

Humane and Patronizing

Your opponents may act humane on the outside but repress behavior that is different than their own. They are friendly until a minority opinion comes up and then will crush anyone standing for an unpopular opinion.

A rule of thumb is to always "feed" the primary process. Feed their humaneness. Support their identity and remind them of it. Compliment them for being humane. Compliment them for being open to new ideas even though they may be temporarily uncomfortable.

Humane groups act egalitarian and may not realize that there is as much power here as any other place on earth. The greater the hope for leaderless and egalitarian groups, the more invisible power usually is. Then speakers are often afraid of their strength and actually need encouragement to stand strongly for the power, for a few temporary dictators could actually give the group the structure it is usually missing.

Festive

Some groups are wild and boisterous or identify themselves with being just plain festive. They are in the midst of gregarious and noisy behavior and refuse to have their party disturbed. If they are disturbed, they will turn nasty.

Feed this monster too. Praise the mood in the air and curse yourself for having to bring up something that is introverted or does not fortify the interactions. Assure them that after you speak you will go right back to the party, and that everyone can return to their merry-making. Do not begin speaking until people agree to let you do so.

Formal

Some groups behave stiffly and formally. They look down on emotions and personal confessions. They have rigid rules of communication. There may be long pauses and painful silences in their style of communication.

Feed their formality. Praise it and encourage them to withhold their emotions. Ask them in a very formal and intellectual manner advice on how to raise new ideas or emotions in the group.

If they are a business group, they undoubtedly feel that emotions are counterproductive and inhibit efficiency and productivity. Feed that identity by advising them that where rational solutions fail, irrational emotions might clear the air and produce greater results. Tell them that their lack of interpersonal skills impedes their overall efficiency.

Feed the group by not pressing the members to go against their own communication styles. Ask everyone to write down their objections or their feedback; do not require them to express their emotions in the group.

Repressive

Certain groups or collectives are overtly dictatorial. They will repress your opinions, ideas, or lifestyle because they lack sufficient familiarity with the issue or because of your color, race, or religion. This is a difficult group with which to deal because they are full of unexpressed internal conflict resulting from their fear of the unknown.

Can you feed them? Tell them that their rules and regulations are obviously there because the members want the best for themselves. But remind them that the fastest way to get the best for themselves is by connecting a tiny bit with different people whom they may indirectly need. Warn them that if they do not try to connect, history will eventually destroy their one-sided attitudes.

Racist

Similar to the repressive group, this group superficially acts friendly and formally but avoids those not like them, believing strangers to be dangerous, immoral, dirty, or worthless. They typically avoid subjects that deal with their viewpoints. They might act open-minded but are deeply closed to new opinions.

You should be careful with this group. Try to determine if you are detached enough from your position to try the following. Begin by being humble. Tell them you have the same desire for security and safety that they do. Try to use their need for security and safety in your favor by hinting that if they heard other opinions or were open to different types of people, their world would actually be safer. Model humility by showing them your own racist opinions.

Religious

A religious group is one in which the members are linked by their beliefs. Beliefs are often only primary processes. This could also be a psychological group that states its beliefs in personal growth. These beliefs need to be addressed, especially if members do not realize their dictatorial tendency.

Use the group's deepest interests and beliefs. Unless this group is awakened to the importance of minority viewpoints, your first step is to respect the primary process. Compliment their religion or beliefs, perhaps by saying something like, "Your beliefs show a lot of love for people. How would this love look in practice in the present moment?"

After addressing the monsters, regardless of the type, check the feedback. Wait for the group's verbal or nonverbal agreement. Wait until they ask to hear your opinion before bringing it up. Otherwise, they will resist your communication style, and your issues may never be heard.

It is important to know the group you are dealing with and to feed its primary process. Pace the primary process; speak its language; use the group's timing. If they are rushed, then you should rush and not take up too much of their time. Otherwise, they will be annoyed. If they do not like to show emotions, then do not force them to divulge their feelings. If you are too upset to appreciate the prevailing group spirit, then let out your antagonism and plan on a fight with the monster.

3. Do Innerwork

It is important to pace the majority group's primary process, to not go against it but keep it intact. If, however, you cannot appreciate their primary process because you are too upset, hurt, and disturbed by it, then you have no choice but to either let out your rage and fight or work on yourself to gain the necessary detachment.

You might find yourself becoming a hero. If so, I suggest that you first work internally. Imagine the heroic act and winning or possibly being hurt or killed in the attempt to stand up for your rights. Go through the entire scene first internally and complete it in a fantasy. Find out how it feels to win or die, maybe even to be forgotten after your death.

4. Take Your Own Side

If working on yourself does not give you the detachment necessary to appreciate the majority's primary process, then you should try to complete the whole project on the outside. This might work if the situation allows for group process.

Be heroic and aware. Report on your dilemma, that you cannot appreciate their group identity and that you know that you might die for standing up for your view. Perhaps others will respond to this. Consider that heroism might be a timespirit for the group or for the times. Let others share this heroic experience too. If all goes well, your work and group tension may temporarily be resolved. If not, there is always a next step: Take your own side in a less dramatic way.

Processing Your Side in Public

Assuming that you have been able to address the monster and feed it, the next step is to take your own side. When you stand up for your side, it is important to realize that you are speaking not only for yourself or your group but also for some members of the majority, and for part of the whole world.

The position you represent in a group is not only your personal material but also the position of a timespirit, specific to that group, place, or time. You cannot be alone in your feelings and views; at least one other member of the majority has to feel as you do. Taking too much of the conflict personally will not be useful for you or for the group. You are a channel for a timespirit. You need to speak up and create a role for your ideas, a role from which you can also detach. If you can also detach from your position, you are more likely to be welcomed as someone who is able to help all parts of the group.

You may also need help in filling your role, and you can ask others if they feel the same way you do. But beware of forcing others to support you publicly. If you notice that no one else stands with you, then bring into your speech the timespirit of fear all minorities have. Mention your fear of being hurt, ostracized, or jailed for bringing up a certain topic. You may want to remember above all not only that you are your own side, race, religion, sex, or color but also that you have all the other parts in you.

5. Switch Roles

When you have taken your own side you will be able to genuinely step out and assist the opposing timespirits with their work. Go back and forth between the minority and majority positions, not forgetting to include neutrality as a position. If you are genuine in your work, the others will feel that you are, above all, interested in the betterment of the whole.

6. *Love*

As you detach from your own role and begin to switch sides, you may feel, like many others before you, a kind of openness and love for everyone. Do not be surprised at the feeling of freedom and pleasure in being alive and in the conflict!

Practice taking all positions and enable the other group members to do the same in order for the whole group to become itself. You have taken a special minority position that models a global future we all want.

Now you may be in the ideal position of being able to listen to all sides. Compassionate listening lies at the root of deep democracy. It is a crucial conflict resolution ability and one of the rarest forms of human behavior. Compassionate listening is not detached and cool but actively empathizes with the minority and understands the majority, the radical, and the conventional as parts of everyone. Compassion realizes, above all, that life is too brief to be stuck in any one side of the whole.

Questions

1. Think about a fantasy you have had in which others do not like you. Is your fantasy a symptom of self-criticism? In what way are you in the role of a minority with others?

2. What minorities exist in your family, group, and city? What are you doing to know these real people?

3. What monster characterizes your family, group, and city? Relax the monster by feeding it first before trying to change it.

NOTE

1. Benyaman Yanoov, *The Pursuit of Peace*, p. xxx.
2. I am thankful to Dr. John Johnson for reminding me how inadequate the term 'minority' is. A conscious person in a 'minority' or unfavored role instantly transforms experience being a 'minor' into a sense of leadership.

CHAPTER 10

Caste and Racial Systems

O f all the problems in the world today, I think that racism and the related problem of tribalism are among the most insidious. Racism may even be worse than poverty, for in my travels around the world I have seen that freedom from discrimination and institutionalized racism makes people happier than money. In this chapter I want to explore racism, the process in which one group feels superior to another because of color, family, religion, language, or the like.

Racism and Tribalism

Racism is a subtle form of misoneism, which is a hatred or intolerance of something new or unknown, resulting in insecurity. The racist is a timespirit that touches all of us. It is someone who feels that her or his own intimate friends and family are best. "Others" are dangerous; they come from different families and have different habits, skin color, or religion. The racist avoids others. In the mind of the racist, the others become scapegoats for all the parts of ourselves that we disavow.

Tribalism is strong in-group loyalty and attachment to one's group or family. Tribalism can be loyalty to one's family or kin, to a group's religious beliefs or practices, or to the very land on which people live. I have heard many Israelis complaining that Arabs are dangerous because they will die to get back the territory that the Israeli Jews won in the Six-Day War. Yet the Arabs say the same of the Israelis. White South Africans cannot understand the blacks' attachment to their land, and the black groups conflict over territorial rights within the townships in South Africa.

Paradoxically, the world has more tolerance for tribalism between people of the same color. We seem to overlook atrocities between groups of the same race, religion, or nationality, but have a harder time overlooking overt crimes of hate or racism between different groups.

Like racism, tribalism is also a timespirit. We all have tribalistic tendencies. When we are in a tribal mood, we will defend our loved ones, our home, or even our car to our death. We mistrust strangers in our neighborhoods, newcomers to our groups, or anyone slightly different from what we know. The more the strangers look or act differently than we do, the more we reject them. C. G. Jung would say they are our shadows.

The Caste System

Some light may be shed on racism by examining the origins of the Indian caste system. The old Indian caste system was a system of sanctioned racism in which people were born into particular strata of society and had to fulfill the jobs and social demands required of them at that level. The caste system stems from the Hindu belief that Brahma, who created the first man, Manu, created all the people of the earth from the various body parts of Manu. From his head came the holiest people, the Brahmins. From the hands of Manu came rulers and warriors, the Kshatriyas. From Manu's thighs came the artisans and craftsmen of the world, the Vaisyas, and from his feet came the laborers, the Sudras, who work for the others.

In Hinduism there are four different castes. Brahmins are priests and philosophers. They study sacred books, are supported by the state, are vegetarians, and bathe twice daily in flowing water. The Kshatriyas govern and perform legal activities. They comprise the upper middle class. The Vaisyas minister to material needs. They are the merchants, farmers, and industrialists. The Sudras serve the rest as workmen, artisans, farm laborers, servants, and gardeners.

The Untouchables

There is another group, the untouchables, who are not supposed to fit into this caste system. They are "subhuman," dangerous, and capable of contaminating members of the other castes. The unhappiness and anger of the untouchables have been the source of many social uprisings in India.

In the Hindu caste system, Manu represents the field, and each caste represents a role or timespirit in this field. There is a spiritual head, a detached role for awareness. The hands are the rulers or government clerks who follow orders. The skilled craftsmen keep the system running, and the workers carry out the menial tasks. There is also a "nonrole" for the untouchables, what I would call *city shadows,* people with whom no one wants to identify. They are the insane, bums, street people, lazy ones, or visionaries.

The whole world treats certain groups of people as untouchables. Their behavior and customs are too different. Refusing to feed or care for them, the majority disregards their plight. Whole groups of people become city shadows for a nation; they are the unwanted part of a global field, the part of the country that people hate to acknowledge.

The caste system describes the roles or organs of a group body and unconsciously identifies people with roles. It creates a value system in which the priests are the best and the untouchables the worst. Since people are equated with the positions, tribalism results.

Identifying people with certain roles over time in a fixed way is racism. No one individual can be only one organ of the anthropos in which we live. Having a personality is more accurately depicted as being the cells in the anthropos's blood. Each cell travels throughout the body. Sometimes we are the feet or workers, sometimes the spiritual mind, sometimes the hands, sometimes the leaders, and also sometimes the untouchables, especially when we get drunk, depressed, or crazy or enter other altered states that are usually ignored. From this viewpoint, tribalism, racism, and segregation are tendencies to identify people with specific timespirits or cultural roles.

Racism as a Timespirit

The field idea sees individuals as roles within a country's field; likewise, countries can occupy roles for an even larger field, the global field. Therefore, we might consider that a country such as South Africa has, until 1990, most easily filled the role of the racist, but it is by no means the only racist country in the global field. "Apartheid," in fact, is a tendency in every country.

In other words, the racial conflict in South Africa has a real locality but is a nonlocal timespirit as well, one that appears wherever people of different tribes, families, religions, colors, and languages hate each other. Thus, there is no way to hide from, ignore, or boycott South Africa, because South Africa is a timespirit that exists everywhere. And like a timespirit, the problem will not be solved by our trying to deny its existence. We cannot clear up the problems of a nonlocal timespirit by working on it in one locality only.

"Manu" is a symbol of the humanlike field in which we live, and wherever we feel a part of a group, community, tribe, city, nation, or world, we generate a Manulike being. Even street people have their own Manulike culture. Those who identify themselves as "tramps" tell me they are better than "bums," who will never work at anything. According to the principle of nonlocality, we can process a distant problem locally by becoming aware of it in our present setting. We live in a world where foreign issues do not exist. The idea that the whole world is within us is no longer simply a transpersonal or archetypal belief: it is a practical and political necessity.

Since we always tend to favor some parts of ourselves over other parts, the beginning of work on racism is recognizing it within ourselves and stating it as clearly as possible to others as well. Only then can we face our own prejudices and become more whole by taking over parts we have disavowed.

This reminds me of a relationship problem I had working with a group in Kenya. In the midst of a group meeting, a black woman told me she was suspicious of whites. I tried to understand her and asked her to forgive me for being white. I reached out, ignoring her suspicion, and asked her to meet me in my reaching out.

She looked away, replying that she did not trust me. "Why do you want to know me better?" she asked suspiciously. I weakly defended myself instead of realizing that she was right to doubt me.

If I could have been completely honest, I would have confessed that I was indeed lying. I was being patronizing and was not really interested in meeting her. She was more honest in her suspicion than I was in my reaching out. I had actually been hurt and angry with her for being suspicious of me. Even though I said I was interested in reaching out, I was secretly thinking that she was being racist toward me because I was white.

Suddenly I felt as if I were in the minority position. I felt inferior and rejected. Knowing this made me feel closer to her. I complained about being segregated, and she laughed. For a split second the black and white timespirits collapsed, and we both became just people again.

I have done better in other places, especially when I was not directly involved. Once when I was working in a racially mixed group, a black man complained about feeling ignored and left out by the rest of the group, mainly white participants. A white man rose at one point and claimed that he did not trust blacks and did not want to be nice to blacks just because they were black!

When I challenged the white man to experiment with the trust he thought he did not have, he said, "I would never turn my back on a black man." I recommended that he try it, and he grudgingly turned his back to his black "adversary." Everyone held their breath to see what would happen between the two men. The black man surprised everyone when he, after a moment's hesitation, embraced the white man.

These men processed the two timespirits in conflict by clearly stating their feelings and then transforming. There they stood, one embracing the other from behind and deeply touching the hundred people in that room. Even people who never hugged anyone in public were moved to do so then and there.

Different parts, like black and white, are not only people but also timespirits. Black, white, Asian, Arab, Israeli, and African are all just people standing for the momentary timespirit.

Paradoxically, by seeing our identities as momentary timespirits, we lose our old identities and simultaneously increase our identity to the entire world. Our attachment to our nationality, sex, race, religion, and age relaxes as our connection to other timespirits increases.

I was born in the United States but have lived much of my life in Europe. Yet I also feel Asian, African, and Australian. I feel Japanese because I had a powerful religious experience in a Zen monastery in Kyoto. I was initiated into African manhood by our healers in the bush outside Mombasa. When I was in India, I had déjà-vu experiences, remembering streets I had never seen.

When I withdraw from the world to the Swiss Alps, my neighbor looks like our next-door neighbor in Oregon. Switzerland and Oregon are not separate places but fields that reproduce themselves wherever we go. In the same way, there is no me, just a transient timespirit brought to birth by a specific field in a certain time and space.

Separatism and Difference

We must be careful, however, not to forget the lines that separate us. Though parts of the world are experiencing unification, there are many other parts that are splitting apart and separating at a rapid rate.

I think of Jerusalem, which today is the holy city of differences. It is divided into fourths, with the Christians, Jews, Armenians, and Arabs each occupying one-fourth of the city. Each quarter is separated by soldiers, guns, and hostility.

In one town, there are four timespirits in conflict, separated by the fear of death. There is a great lesson in Jerusalem. Despite the world's quest for peace and unity, there is an equal and important quest for difference. Unity and harmony may also be ideals that tyrannize ethnic centricity. Jerusalem reminds us that before we can have unity, we need to clearly define the timespirits and the roles in the field. We need to value tribalism, the need to belong to a specific tribe. We need to support the drive to belong to a locale, community, and group. People need to feel at home, special, and unique before they can be requested to unite with others.

Racism, seen in this respect, is a violent overcompensation for the tyranny of unity and harmony, which has no respect for differences.

Processing Racial or Religious Tensions

Since each of us is responsible for resolving racial tensions, I think we should all participate in solving or processing some of the racial and religious tensions and conflicts typical of the Middle East. Imagine being in the following situation.

You are in an airport, boarding a domestic flight in Israel. Passengers are asked to go through special security procedures. Black-clad Orthodox Jews move into a corner near the window to pray. A fellow passenger, a secular Jew, leans toward you and complains to you about the "Palestinian problem." She says that the Palestinians devote their life to killing Jews. What do you say to her?

The airport security is tight. A constant fear of terrorism is in the air. Heavily armed airport police are inspecting passengers for weapons and bombs. They thoroughly inspect the men in the men's bathroom and the women in the women's bathroom. Where is the evil one? The terrorist?

At the Tel Aviv airport, you take a taxi to your hotel, and the taxi driver, hearing that you are European, complains that the Europeans are anti-Semitic because they support the Palestinians. How do you feel? What do you say to him?

You go out to dinner, and your waiter is Palestinian. He tells you not to believe the Israelis because they all lie. They do not want the tourists to know how much tension and trouble there is. Suddenly, he looks around and becomes afraid that an undercover agent will see him talking to you. He is afraid of being beaten up and interrogated.

Depressed and saddened by what you have seen and heard, you go outside and look at the beautiful Mediterranean, but you see blood, not water, there. What are the timespirits in this field? How will you help the situation? What will you say or do? What do you feel?

Imagine that on your way home your worst fear comes true: your plane is hijacked by a terrorist. Are you prepared? Remember that terrorists are furious. They will blame everyone, including innocent children, for their situation. The terrorist does not abide by humanistic motives. He will not use direct confrontation but prefers guerrilla warfare and terrorist tactics. He will sacrifice his own life for his beliefs. He is fighting for an ideal. The timespirit of the terrorist is violent and fights for the sake of his God. Where is he?

My political platform is a theory of history. Everyone is partially responsible for cocreating our global field. Everyone who lives in or experiences racial tensions or conflicts such as I have described above is partially responsible for them. In fact, anyone who even hears about such incidents is responsible. Even if you only see a racial or terrorist incident on television, you are responsible for it because your reactions are part of the overall tension waiting to be processed.

If you deny the terrorist timespirit in yourself, if you allow yourself to live only as a nice person and repress your spontaneous tendency to conflict, confront, and stand for your highest principles, if you avoid potentially fiery interactions, then others will have to occupy this timespirit. And there are no guarantees that they will do it more consciously than you.

Racial problems cannot be solved only where they are most obvious. Nothing can be solved only in one locality, with one group, in a world of global fields. Innerwork on conflicts, as well as local and global group work must all go together.

Questions

1. When did you last feel like a terrorist?

2. Were you an untouchable in your group?

3. What can you do to resolve minority issues and terrorist behavior around you or in your group?

4. Identify prejudices against a group which you have now or have had in the past. Where did you learn this prejudice?

5. In what way do you sometimes behave like the group against which you are prejudiced?

6. Consider the possibility that this group is an aspect of yourself. How could you use more of this group behavior in your behavior? How should you be using less of it?

CHAPTER 11

Women and Men

I believe that the Third World War has been going on since the early part of the twentieth century. The Third World War is the war between women and men. Women all over the world are awakening to themselves, and many are furious with men who represent rigid patriarchal views. Men as well are just beginning to awaken to the value and depth of their natures, and some feel that women are responsible for repressing ancient and important male values. These conflicts are almost universal, we find them in the United States, Europe, Africa, Japan, and India.

The male-female conflict looks like Manu's problem: one part of the anthropos is favored over another. Why have typical masculine values been favored over femininity by so many of us? Why do businesses pay women less money than they pay men? Why do more men than women study at universities? Why are women blamed for destroying the home life when they want to go out and work, as they are doing in America, Europe, and especially Africa? Why are girl babies still killed in China, or wives burned in India for failing to bring enough dowry to the marriage? Why are so many modern men in the United States and Europe afraid to be wild and powerful; where has the sound of their drums gone?

All over the world, women bear the brunt of the burden of maintaining relationships and family and social structures. In many countries, women are also contributing substantially, if not solely, to financial support. Men feel they have no feelings if they are not able to express themselves in the same ways as women.

Wherever we work, the male-female problem appears. Whether we are working on racial tensions, on community problems, or in businesses, the group either splits overtly on the male-female issue, or suffers quietly with the background tension. In most parts of the world, except for psychological workshops in parts of Europe and America, women rarely speak in public. And in some parts of the United States, Australia, and Europe, women explode in rage at men as men continue to harbor deep suspicions about the nature of women.

The gender conflict is structurally similar to racial and class conflict, since in each case one role is evaluated as better than another, and individuals are equated with either preferred or rejected roles. But racism differs from sexism in that sexism is independent of race, religion, nationality, or family.

In psychological groups, the conflict between men and women tends to polarize around two different roles: fact versus feeling, business versus relationship, doing versus being, head versus heart, leader versus follower. These roles are timespirits; all of us have both poles within us.

Currently, in the United States, Europe, and Australia, the psychotherapeutic and medical establishments are beginning to react to sexual abuse. Yet not enough realize the political consequences of psychology's subtle devaluation of women. Certain psychological schools fall prey to sexist attitudes by attempting to work with women's unhappiness and anger as if these feelings were solely women's psychological problems.

Trying to change people because you cannot get along with their behavior or implying a client should work on a problem internally without requiring yourself or the culture to change the problem is patronizing at best. At worst, it is a hierarchical statement that you are superior, and it is a hypnotic induction guaranteed to make the other feel inferior. What is ridiculous about this common psychological procedure is that the therapist is usually avoiding his or her feelings about a client. Thus, if a woman or man becomes too violent, it is easier for a therapist to think she or he is one-sided than it is for him to tell the client that he does not like the way she or he is and to face the resulting encounter.

Many therapists may even propagate problems by using the language of opposites, which secretly contains the message that differences may be unresolvable. There is a time for seeing individuals and the world as roles, and there is a time for looking directly at one another, independent of roles and culture, and saying, "You are hurting me."

In the past, I, too, have used my head instead of my heart. I remember a woman once screaming at me in a seminar that she hated men because they were so loud. I used my rational, psychological abilities, and, as calmly and quietly as I could, told her that I did not like loud men either, whether they appeared as women or men.

She got the point and instantly quieted down, but she never talked to me again. I felt I had won and was proud of myself. But what had I won?

I had used my psychological abilities against her. In retrospect, I now realize that even though I cleverly pointed out to her how noisy *she* was, *I* became the very man she hated. I was not humble enough to admit to her that, when she attacked me, I wanted to overcome her and "win" the interaction. I wanted to enlighten her at least as much as she wanted to change me! Why did I have to win? Why did I not just cry when she screamed at me?

I myself had no access to the parts that I felt were missing in her! I was missing humility. My unconscious insistence upon winning was chauvinistic. I proved her correct by putting her down in a typically "male" fashion.

I feel bad about that scene even as I write about it today. I realize now that anyone who tries to win through the use of force, anyone who seeks to be more enlightened than someone else, anyone who is interested in teaching someone who has not asked to be taught is unfortunately and unconsciously occupying the tyrannical spirit of a field.

The next time a group process occurred, I had learned more about the male-female conflict and was more conscious and prepared. This time it was in Europe. A woman stood up in a group process class in Zurich and correctly criticized many of my colleagues for using masculine pronouns. She was right. Some of our European trainers had not yet learned about gender-corrected pronouns. They admitted their mistakes, yet the process continued. It became a power struggle, and some members of the group tried to pull the woman down by proving that she was being "masculine" in her insensitivity.

In the midst of this collective issue, I suddenly felt compelled to speak personally about my own experiences. I grew up in a world where women were treated as being less important than men. No one ever said this overtly to me when I was a child, but I felt it. No one explained to me why one of my uncles was given a college education because he was the oldest male in the family, while my mother, who was actually the oldest child, had to sew to support his college education! Why? Why did he not sew to support her education?

My reflections momentarily resolved the group process because someone simply admitted unconsciousness about the conflict. Picking up the one who merely listened, suffered, and admitted unconsciousness was important. For once, I was not fighting "man to man" but simply accepting and suffering over the situation. Sometimes, however, a personal admission is insufficient because it fails to represent the rest of the group. The field itself wants to go deeper into the problem.

Some months later, the same issue arose again in a Portland group, and again it cycled painfully. No matter what happened, there was no settling the problem. My wife, Amy, and I, completely at a loss as to how to resolve the conflict, decided to experiment with creating a group theater. We thought that since people continued to tell painful stories of mistreatment toward women, we could ritualize the unresolved process. We introduced the idea that since the discussion could not be resolved by ordinary means, we might examine it in greater detail by using a theater approach. We invited the others to take part. Amy and I stood up and went into the center of the room, where we improvised a theater, portraying the brutality to which we had been listening.

Spontaneously others stood up and created their own scenes from what we had heard. The improvisations evolved into groups of threes: one player was the "man," one was the "woman," and one was an observer who intervened into the conflict when he or she felt compelled to do so.

Dozens of such triads performed, one after another, demonstrating the infinite number of variations and solutions to the painful conflict we had been discussing.

At the end of the group process theater someone sang a song, improvising the words as well. The words, to the best of my recollection, went something like this:

This has been the group process theater
look at it and enjoy
suffer and wonder
and watch yourself go unconscious once again
choosing as you always do
to forget what you have just learned
opting for unconsciousness instead of creativity.

The male-female conflict must come up again and again until we have exhausted its feeling and content. In a San Francisco group process that happened just days before the 1989 earthquake, a woman rose and spoke out wisely and angrily against rape.

This started a nasty group process. Blame, accusations, guilt, and denial went back and forth for what seemed like ages. Suddenly, a realization occurred to me. Why not just listen? First I, and then slowly many other men, stood quietly, one after the other, and listened to the women's pain.

When the women were finished, one man after another spoke about his pain as well. Here was the same conflict with a brand new twist. It became neither a men's nor a women's group but a public hearing in which all were able to hear the feelings of the others.

The next morning, however, one woman criticized me for having tried to avoid some of the first outraged cries against the men. I could only admit my guilt. She was right. I had simply wanted to avoid pain. I had been through so many scenes of conflict and seen so much brutality and pain cycle endlessly that I had just had enough.

I told the woman that the conflict I had experienced was so painful that sometimes I could barely take it anymore, that sometimes I did not feel completely up to the challenge and wanted to avoid it. Although I know how important it is to allow pain and anger to be aired, I sometimes just hurt from the brutality.

After saying that, I just cried. When the woman saw me cry, something changed for her, and she asked how she could formulate her statements in a way that would cause less pain. I could not think of anything to say. For once I was silent, thankful to her for helping me discover my feelings.

Treatises and Resolutions

We must carefully attend to the way in which we complete and resolve conflicts. If both sides gain some insight, all goes well. If only one side wins, both lose.

Consider the Treaty of Versailles, which ended the First World War. Under pressure from the French, the treaty became a harsh punishment against the defeated Germans. Large land areas had to be transferred to the sovereignty of other nations; the Germans had to pay enormous reparations and suffered economically and psychologically.

The humiliation of Germany may have inspired the thirst for revenge, the desire for power and conquest that was the hallmark of the Nazi party. It was in an atmosphere of punishment and cruelty that the Nazi party was born. Germany was forced to redeem itself in another war.

Think of the contrasting Marshall Plan, which helped reconstruct the European economy, devastated by the Second World War. The Marshall Plan was highly successful and contributed to the rapid renewal of the European industries.

Similarly, the treaty with Japan following the Japanese surrender in World War II was a considerate and humane agreement. The status of Emperor Hirohito went untouched, and United States intervention into the everyday life of Japan was kept to a minimum. That country was demilitarized, and the Japanese military was not put on trial. Moreover, economic assistance was given to Japan during the transition time from war to peace.

Both Japan and Germany have become pillars of economic recovery in the West and have remained close allies of the United States and Britain.

The conflict between women and men has been a contested issue for almost a century yet is just beginning to be recognized as a real and valid problem. Hence, we must continue to support the issues as well as the anger and pain involved in the struggle. The war can be shortened by encouraging the battles, especially in areas of the world where the feminist movement has just begun. Perhaps it will help if we all listen to women's voices and realize that they are speaking about feelings that we all have.

In this conflict, neither men nor women can win, for history teaches that no one can truly win a battle unless each shares in the economic, emotional, and moral support of the other.

We must be careful about undermining the male world, because a peace treaty that humiliates and punishes one side too severely will be paid for at another time by another war. Thus, even though the ancient rigid male way will eventually be defeated, it must nevertheless be appreciated and the power within it used for useful purposes.

The temporary cessation of the male-female battle can only happen when there is global appreciation of all minority groups, when we arrive at the deepest level of all, where there is neither male nor female, neither Yin nor Yang, just the awareness of change. Process work could be of use at this point because in principle it is politically neutral. It avoids categorizing and typologizing and understands people as eternally changing. For this reason, however, it may be weak in appreciating the emphasis we sometimes place on our differences.

It is helpful to listen carefully to the way in which we identify as men and women, black and white, Asian and European, Christian and Jew. A process attitude, however, does not fasten to these identities but appreciates them as momentary images that we and the world around us fasten to. Identity is meaningful and can even be a matter of life and death. But like all images, identities are not static pictures but gates to an even more numinous and unknown spirit. It is easy to think this way if we remember that we are all going to die one day and that the dreaming spirit of life that moves us is independent of beauty and time, gender and age, life and maybe even death.

Exercise

1. Remember the last time you or someone else thought a woman was not as valuable as a man.

2. Imagine the kind of woman who was being discussed. What does she look like? How might she act?

3. How are you like this person? Think about this until you have an answer.

4. Imagine how the world or business would change if the woman could be the leader there. What advantages could she bring?

5. Now consider your own work in the world and imagine the advantages that would come about if this woman's way were added.

6. What emotional changes happen to you as you imagine this difference?

7. Contribute to settling the Third World War by changing the way you do business and by allowing gender issues to arise among your friends.

8. What "male role" behavior do you reject? Could you possibly employ such behavior usefully?

CHAPTER 12

City Streets and Ecology

When my wife, Amy, and I were in Bombay, we stopped at a little shop on a back street for something to eat. We each had a Pepsi and a banana, and after we finished them, we looked around for a garbage can. We asked the shopkeeper where to throw our trash. He did not answer but took the cans and banana peels from us and threw them in the street.

Amy and I looked at each other, troubled by this. Bombay was filthy, and our first instinct was to clean up the place, not contribute to its filth by throwing garbage directly into the street. If this was the way things were done in Bombay, I had to ask myself just how much of the city's field I could tolerate.

Before I had an answer, a cow and a young child came by. The cow ate the banana peels, and the child picked up the cans and some other trash from the gutter and walked on. I suddenly realized that there was no trash; most everything in the gutter could be reused, eaten, or resold.

Now I had my answer. Nothing can be thrown out of a field. We are all truly interconnected as one being. I was initially shocked when I saw the shopkeeper throw the banana peels and cans into the street. But when I saw the child and the cow pick up and use these things, I saw that there is an ecology to every field.

Was throwing the cans and peels into the street creating pollution, or was it ecological? If the shopkeeper had not thrown them into the street, the boy would have had no aluminum to sell and would probably have been even hungrier, and the cow that ate the banana peels would have been weaker as well.

How do we define that complex interaction whose final outcome spells ecology? Ecological thinking must by nature include psychology, spirituality, and politics. When this connection between spirituality, planetary health, and politics occurs, we shall be living in a new world.

Ecology and Health

I used to think about health and healing in terms of eating the right food, getting plenty of exercise, and being in good psychological shape. But I have increasingly moved away from monocausal thinking about health.

Caffeine is typically seen as a harmful drug that overexcites the nervous system, complicates high blood pressure and digestion, can be harmful to the intestines, and contributes to lumps in the breasts. However, under certain circumstances, drinking coffee can be useful.

I remember a client years ago who was in the last stages of terminal cancer. She came in complaining that she was extremely depressed and could not sleep at night, in spite of medication. Suspecting that her sleep disorder might be supporting a need to stay up, I decided to follow the process that was happening. I recommended that she drink black coffee before bed. At least, I argued, she would be able to complete all her business and income taxes before her death.

The woman willingly drank her coffee and stayed up at night. She not only did her taxes but also wrote a number of articles for magazines. She started to sleep in the afternoons. After a few weeks, a strange thing happened. Her cancer stopped growing, and she stopped chemotherapy treatments. The cancer did not reverse but did not progress either. She finished writing the articles and submitted them to be published. After they were accepted and published, she made a complete recovery.

There is no way, of course, of knowing the reason for the woman's full recovery. Was it luck, my love and belief in her, the chemotherapy, or a spirit reversal, as witch doctors would say? I would like to pretend that the coffee was good "ecology"; it followed her total life process.

Human systems cannot be helped in only a monocausal fashion. Our world is just too complex. Caffeine is a known toxin, a drug that is supposed to be harmful. In fact, many people try to reduce their consumption of coffee because of caffeine's harmful effects. Yet, for this woman, in this situation, it might have been just the medicine she needed. It mirrored her secondary process; it supported the natural events happening to her. However, drinking coffee without getting to work would be just plain harmful. Good ecology means following the overall process by using the state of mind. It was not only using a substance that worked; the woman made an attitude shift as well.

Good ecology means deep democracy, that is, mindfully fathoming what is trying to happen, appreciating it, analyzing it with both rapture and a critical mind, and helping the total process unfold.

Could we extend this analogy and think that some of the things we consider toxins might be useful for people or for the earth? Let us consider a community process in terms of ecology. I have been part of several processes in which the consciousness of a group seemed connected with synchronistic effects in a given bioregion. One of the most dramatic events happened while we were at Esalen, in Big Sur, California, during our first residency there.[1]

Ecology and Synchronistic Effects

The weather, land, and psychology at Esalen seemed to connect one fall evening in 1988. The community had been on the brink of change since the death of one of its leaders, Dick Price. The different factions were in disagreement with one another, and conflicts were rampant. In order to try to set things on the right track again, the managers asked a series of resident teachers to come into Esalen from the outside.

Amy and I were invited to be the first residents in the program. At the time of our arrival at Esalen, Big Sur and most of California were suffering from a drought. Conditions were particularly severe, and the autumn rains had not yet arrived.

The community, too, had been in a sort of a drought. Tensions were running high. When we arrived, we decided to begin our residency by calling a meeting for the entire community. Rarely had the entire community, which includes scholars, trainers, managers, workers, and visitors, met at once. We called the meeting for a Wednesday evening at 7:30 P.M. As the residents began to gather in the big conference room, it started to rain.

The rain was so gentle at first that no one noticed it. Suddenly, just as the meeting began, the heavens opened up, and rain poured down on the Big Sur community. It only rained that night in the area around

Big Sur, including a stretch of coastline about forty miles north of Esalen and another stretch about thirty-five miles south.

Was there a synchronistic connection between the two atmospheres—the human system and the earth—or was it all just coincidental? Perhaps the spirit of the place, the earthspirit, had been dry and in need of release and resolution. If I had been more awake, I would have brought the earth into the work, as a troubled timespirit of the moment in the group process.

The event reminded me of the Taoist rainmaker story told by Richard Wilhelm to C. G. Jung.[2] In this story, a region in China was suffering from a terrible drought. The people of the region decided to call on the Taoist rainmaker to come and make it rain. When he arrived, he looked around and asked for a hut where he could go by himself.

He went up to the hut and sat inside. After one day, nothing had happened. After the second day, nothing had happened. On the evening of the third day, it began to rain and continued to do so into the next day. Later, when the rainmaker left his hut and came down the hill, Wilhelm asked him how he had done it. The rainmaker replied that he had done nothing at all. He had just noticed that the people of the village were not in Tao, so he put himself in Tao and it rained. For him, the region was a field, a bioregion, an unknown spirit that included everything in the neighborhood. The difference between the Esalen and the Taoist story is that the whole community in Esalen tried to get itself into Tao.

Good Ecology

Good ecology means living congruently with the earth, and this depends upon our ability to get into Tao, to follow the energy of the field we are in. Perhaps even our very attempt at Esalen to solve problems, to align ourselves with the powers in the neighborhood, sufficed.

What it means for a community, as for an individual, to live in Tao is to live congruently with access to all parts. If a community has a lot of emotional tension that has been dammed up, then merely creating an outlet for the release of the emotions enables the community to be more congruent. Opening up emotionally and falling rain are not all that different.

Practicing good ecology means going with the unexpected and neglected parts of the environment. In earthquake country, for example, it could mean noticing what is trying to rumble and making an attempt to bring neglected things up to an otherwise sunny surface. Living congruently with an accident such as an oil spill could mean using less oil. The meaning of a given incident is entirely dependent upon the group or individual perceiving and being affected by it. The important issue is trying to derive some meaning out of a strange incident.

Good ecology uses everything, including banana peels, Pepsi cans, and emotions. We need to recycle everything we use, neglecting and throwing away nothing. Ordinary feelings you have while walking down the street are sacred. What makes living valuable is the sense of meaningfulness that comes from the ability to derive value from everything, even things that at first look destructive.

To practice good ecology, we have to follow the neglected, the unpredictable, the numinous, and everything that catches our eye. This means thinking about the planet as we think about our own bodies, our dreams, our families, and our groups. It means supporting minority opinions, standing for the inaudible and the awesome. It means bravely diving into a troublesome field, pulling it into pieces, and then letting its own wisdom show us how to put it together again. It means not being wise but letting the wisdom of the group emerge; it means facilitating, not only leading.

The Leaders Must Die

Esalen suffered the agony of any little planet in search of its wholeness. Many of its best leaders had died. Fritz Perls was gone. Virginia Satir had just died. Harry Sloan had died, and Dick Price had been recently killed. What wisdom could the Tao possibly have in mind for all the leaders to die? Not only in Esalen but also all over the world we find a lack of leaders, an absence of good leadership. Where are the world's leaders?

Field theory helps us understand where the leaders are. We project our wholeness onto individual women and men who are actually not up to our projections. The leaders are not bad or inferior, but leadership is a role, a timespirit that can only be filled by all of us. The best leader is at best only a facilitator for the wisdom already inherent in a group.

There can be no single rainmaker. The idea of there being a best leader must die, because it takes away the responsibility and awareness of what needs to be done by each individual. The idea of a great leader is crippling, because the real leader is any individual, anywhere and anytime, who is aware of the type of process trying to happen and who makes room for it to happen. Leaders are those who use their awareness to divine the Tao.

Earth Service

Good ecology is not just having clean air, water, and earth. It also involves our awareness of what processes are trying to happen. Good ecology becomes what I call earth service when we have the courage to follow these processes. Earth service means helping individuals and groups become their individual and total selves. Awakening groups to the significance and power in their symptoms and problems and reversing their attitudes toward these problems can also reverse the apparently negative effects of the problem.

Being loving, thinking positive thoughts, and honoring others and the land are necessary but not sufficient. If service to the earth becomes a single and simple preaching, no one will follow it. Who wants to honor others if they are cruel? I will not honor anything, even Mother Earth, if she kills us in the same way we destroy the environment.

Earth service is a much more complex business than being loving and serving! It is a matter of awareness of all parts. Earth service will always be an individual matter. One person or group will follow the Tao by setting altars and praying, while others must stamp their feet and shovels on the ground! All of our reactions and feelings and the interactions between them are the Tao.

Serving the earth will mean reversing history, reversing the unthinkable amount of unconsciousness, pain, and meaningless tension that has always gone hand in hand with world processes. We need to cocreate history by noticing what is trying to happen and assisting it before it repeats itself and overwhelms us.

Portland's Street People

To test this viewpoint about the importance of the minority, at a recent class in Portland about the homeless I decided to interview and work with street people. With the help of the process work staff there, I worked with any street person who happened to pass the lecture hall at the time of the class. My experiences verified the generally accepted statistics, which show that one-third of the homeless are deinstitutionalized mentally ill, one-third are addicted to drugs or alcohol, and one-third reflect the changing economic and social policies of the government. The painful story of poverty is barely realized by the rest of the country, which ignores the struggles of its millions of street people.

But even less known are the inner experiences of our beggars. Many are so severely drugged or in altered states of consciousness that the very belief that being normal means earning a living seems crazy from their viewpoint! In such circumstances, where people feel they are well and the rest of the world is crazy, my approach is to learn from the city's shadow.

For example, one chronic drunk laughed at my class. He insisted that only he was truly free. After all, he traveled by freightcar going north in the summer and south in the winter. Home, he told us, was the moment. Another agreed. Home was where God let him fall at night. Still another blessed everyone all the time. Another apparently schizophrenic man told us that he too was free; after all, he was an American, he said, and could come and go as he needed. A wild street person whom one of our process workers interviewed on a street screamed, while carrying a bag on his back, that "the war is here now, here now, here now!" The war, he tried to explain, was due to throwing out food. After thinking about that, I understood that all these street people were our potential food or nourishment which we are throwing out. Aspects of their lifestyle are needed by everyone.

While doing process work with a street person during one of our television shows in Portland, a man called Tennessee said, in a drunken stupor, that God was on his side and not on the side of the police, who tried to clear street people away from the stores in order to make way for the shoppers. He explained his drinking by saying that, after all, Jesus turned water into wine; therefore, he was a religious man and free of guilt.

Street people need our help and love, but we must not just patronize them. Good ecology and deep democracy mean not throwing out the spiritual food these street teachers have for us. It only seems that we live in a world where spiritual teachers are disappearing. Closer inspection shows that many of our newest transpersonal teachers live in altered states of consciousness right on our city streets. Life itself seems to have taught them to know that this moment is our true home and that the best place to search for the true self is in the garbage can of unused experience.

Exercise

1. Next time you are in town, sit down near a street person and imagine that she is your teacher from whom you may benefit.

2. Give her a few dollars.

3. Ask her about her experiences on the street, the good and bad parts.

4. Learn from those people and parts of the earth you cannot immediately change.

5. Choose part of your immediate physical environment which you do not like very much. Perhaps it is a piece of dirt or plastic or decaying wood. Focus upon it, and experiment with the fantasy of becoming the object.

6. "Clean it up" by asking how you are already too much like this part of the environment and how you might possibly recycle or use this part of yourself better.

NOTES

1. This story is described in greater detail in Mindell, *Riding the Horse Backwards.*

2. See C. G. Jung, *The Collected Works,* vol. 14, *Mysterium Coniunctionus.*

PART IV

THE POSSIBLE UNIVERSE

CHAPTER 13

Mind Reversal and Healing

The last chapters have shown that we have the capacity to experience ordinary life more fully than we do. Conflict, gender differences, pollution, and minority issues can turn painful situations into awesome challenges. The ability to live with awareness and compassion in our everyday life is one of the goals of deep democracy.

We know from field theory that the way we live and process intense experiences, whether they be symptoms, dreams, relationship issues, group dynamics, or the political, ecological, and historical events around us, influences the future of the world. The final chapters of this book discuss the influence of awareness and consciousness upon healing, magic, and the future of the world.

Going Backward in Time

How many times have you thought about someone and then bumped into them, or received a phone call or letter from them? C. G. Jung called this type of occurrence a synchronicity, or meaningful coincidence between two otherwise disconnected events. Whether you believe in synchronicity or coincidence and luck, inner experiences and events often seem the same as outer events.

In *Journey to Ixtlan,* Carlos Castaneda tells a story about himself and his shaman-mentor, Don Juan. Carlos and Don Juan were walking through a busy marketplace in a Mexican town one day, when Carlos panicked after seeing an acquaintance whom he had been trying to avoid. Don Juan noticed his apprentice's unfortunate predicament and pushed him out of the way by giving him a solid blow on the back. Rather than just pushing Carlos out of the thoroughfare, the blow pushed him backward in time.

Carlos suddenly found himself walking through the marketplace of that same Mexican town a week earlier. When Carlos "came to" from this experience, he returned to that marketplace and was able to verify that the market and all the people had indeed been where they had been in his vision, even though he had not been there in reality.

The Feynman Model of Electrons in a Field

The reader can view this as a parable, a description of a parapsychological event, or merely as fiction. I am fascinated by how a model of such apparently parapsychological events may be found in modern physics in Richard Feynman's theory of antimatter.[1] In the 1960s, Feynman, who recently won a Nobel Prize for his work, postulated a theory predicting that matter could go backward in time. According to the Feynman theory, developed to explain the behavior of elementary particles in a magnetic field, an electron going forward in time can reverse itself.

Feynman's theory concerned electrons, microscopic particles of matter with negative electrical charges, and positrons, similar to electrons but with positive electrical charges. Physicists call positrons "antimatter" because they are like electrons but are more rare and live for very short lengths of time. In psychological terms, we might think of the electron as "real" and the positron as "dreamlike."

Feynman's theory explains the behavior of matter when it runs into a magnetic field. The existing explanation at that time was that an electron travels forward in time until it runs into a strong magnetic field. The magnetic field influences the electron, which develops a pair, a new electron and a "double," or positron. Now there are three particles, the original electron, and the electron and positron pair created through interaction with the field.

According to the explanation, the positron that was created as part of the pair when the original electron entered the magnetic field goes along in time with the original electron and eventually annihilates both itself and that electron. Finally, the electron from the pair goes on as if it were the reincarnation of the original one in another form.

Feynman thought about this and predicted that an entirely different explanation could also be possible. When the electron ran into the magnetic field, he said, it did not necessarily have to create a new electron-positron pair and eventually be annihilated but could remain intact without creating a double and without being annihilated.

All we had to do, according to Feynman's second interpretation, is to imagine that the original electron, in traveling through the magnetic field, reverses itself in time. It travels backward in time, eventually reverses itself again, goes forward in time, and finally emerges from the magnetic field.

Developing a Double

Thus, physics postulates possible interpretations to explain the behavior of an elementary particle when it runs into a magnetic field. One interpretation is that it develops a dreamlike double, and the other is that it remains itself and reverses itself in time. If we use physics as an analogy for human behavior, we can think of the original electron as a person entering a particularly intense field that has an effect on that individual.

Like the electron, when we run into a difficult situation, we have two choices. We can become split personalities, become incongruent, and develop a dreamlike double as we try to continue being normal, or we can step out of time, so to speak, and sort of navigate the field and remain ourselves.

What does it mean to develop a double? When we meet an intense situation, like Carlos Casteneda, who ran into someone he wanted to avoid, we begin to *double signal;* that is, we are momentarily split into parts. One part wants to maintain our identity. We try to continue according to plan, to remain normal. But other parts, impulses, and emotions arise, and we become incongruent. We emit a number of conflicting messages and signals. Like Carlos, we are not fluid, and we split off the feelings and parts that do not go along with our intentions. Thus, we develop complexes, body symptoms, dreams, and fantasies, all of which I call secondary processes.

Our bodies begin to go crazy, creating numerous messages and confusing everyone. We develop a double. One part is the ordinary self, and the other part is a dreamlike self, carrying a conflicting message and causing us problems. Like the positron, it disturbs, upsets, or even annihilates us, our normal identity and intent.

In other words, dreamlike phenomena knock out our rigid identities and create altered states, disturbances, symptoms, hallucinations, dreams, and disturbing thoughts. They can even endanger our health by causing accidents. Unconscious behavior becomes self-destructive without consciousness.

Time and Mind Reversal

Rather than being annihilated by secondary processes, the fluid warrior can use her awareness and allow herself to change her identity. She can consciously decide that her intent is not the only path and can instead follow the lead of what is happening. The more aware and fluid she is, the more she can ride the energies of the field, the lines of force of her city and time. Whenever she enters a particularly intense situation, she notices the timespirits. Instead of allowing them to create dreams, body symptoms, or relationship troubles that threaten her identity, she goes with them, changing her identity, and thus stepping out of time and into the Tao.

Going backward in time means leaving primary processes behind. It means leaving our normal agenda, our plans, intentions, conscious goals. When disturbances hit, or when a situation impinges upon our awareness, rather than simply surging forward, we let go and follow the secondary processes, going with the timespirits that are present.

Going backward in time is practicing dying, practicing giving up our goals, intentions, and identity, and following the path of the dreaming processes. To do this is to metaphorically die, to give up who we are, and to identify with the overall changes. My experiences with many dying clients leave me with the impression that the lesson of many real deaths seems to be letting go and becoming one with the Tao.[2] According to theory, we need not wait till death to go backward in time, to step out of our ordinary identities.

Thus, the new leader, like a spiritual warrior, reverses body symptoms and problems and goes out of linear time, perhaps even backward in time, into earlier periods to find parts of herself and her community that are trying to arise now. If the warrior fluidly allows herself to die by letting herself move in and out of her identity, she goes backward and forward in time by following the body feelings and the fantasies and intuitions she has.

Inner Experiences and Outer Events

Amy and I were skiing in the mountains, trekking along the steep sides of a remote valley. We were alone, as very few other skiers ever ski in this particular area of the mountains. As we descended, I found myself in the midst of an internal dialogue, thinking about a child with whom I had worked that week. I was, so to speak, caught in a "magnetic" field.

During the last session, I had been stern with the little girl, confronting her gently with the necessity of having to grow up. I had been extremely coddling and nurturing with her up until the last session, and now a part of me felt unsure about what I had done. I felt guilty for having been stern with her.

I noticed how engaged I was in the internal discussion and suspected that I was in some sort of field, in the cross fire between timespirits. So I stopped where I was and asked Amy for help. I processed the conflict internally and voiced the feelings of the little girl. She wanted the father to be sweeter! The father, however, reversed the girl's feelings by showing her that to be loving might also mean that you sometimes have to be stern.

I felt relieved and was happy with this insight. As we started to ski again, a couple of other skiers appeared on the horizon. This was a bit unusual, as the area is so remote. As they came closer, to our surprise we noticed that it was a father and a little girl. The father was warmly encouraging the girl and giving her tips about her skiing.

I suddenly had the feeling that my innerwork and the outer events collided. I no longer just had an inner dilemma but was in the midst of a field where two timespirits were battling over educating children. How could we explain this? One theory would say that this coincidence was a synchronicity. A fantasy full physicist would say that I had entered a difficult field and developed a double at another point in space. We might also say that I was dreaming about a parent and child and dreamed it up in the outer world. Or should I have stepped "out of time" and become a child?

In any case, we must consider the possibility that innerwork is global work. It is connected to the field in which we live. When one works on the timespirits of a given field, there is no longer an inner-work or outer work, a local or global event. Doing worldwork means being ecological about everything we think, perceive, remember, feel, and fantasize. What we consider our own psychological material is a timespirit in today's world.

Global Meanings and Coupled Events

What role does monocausal thinking play in the example of the little girl just described? Even without the laws of physics, we know that there is a basic symmetry in our universe, though there is no way of knowing who or what is responsible for events.

Did I "cause" the father and child to appear at the moment I was working internally? Is a relationship conflict caused because I moved away from you, or because you moved away from me? Did I attack you, or did I dream the night before that someone attacked me? Did my dreams create my body problems, or do my symptoms create my dreams? Did the problems between Iraq and Kuwait influence the group process in California, or did the California process influence events in the Middle East?

Though there may be moments when it is useful and even necessary to trace the origins and effects of events, we are living in a universe in which all events are coupled to one another in a symmetrical fashion. Thus, we cannot tell what events cause each other, only that connected processes happen to us.

This way of thinking is different than the way we normally approach life, but it leads to an enlarged concept of the self. We normally identify ourselves with only some of our experiences. The other experiences that we think are "not me" then become secondary. They become timespirits and the mysterious world. Yet when we become fluid participants in nature, we are not just the victims of the world's mysterious forces. We are also the mysterious timespirits and forces themselves. If we reverse our normal way of thinking, we realize that we are either a universe in conflict that impinges upon itself or one incredible being with many faces and times. We are a standing invitation and challenge for others to change.

We can continue as we have thus far, trying to change our personal difficulties and the world's problems. Or we can use the disturbances, pollutions, conflicts, and problems and ride the energy and timespirits around us, using this global workshop to become our entire selves. If we continue as we are going now, we will eventually be demolished by the very world we have created, just as the electron is annihilated by its double. If, however, we notice our annihilation coming, we can reverse the trend and annihilate our own identities, thereby becoming anything and everything as the moment requires! This is perhaps what life has in mind for us, both as individuals and as communities. Life is asking us to use the energy and spirit of people and problems we feel are against us. All we have to do is change or reverse our ideas of who we are.

Time Reversibility Exercise

1. Use all your senses and wait patiently for the next intense field situation to arise.

2. Notice body feelings. Watch your mood, dreams, relationships, and the world around you.

3. As soon as the field begins to disturb you or give you the feeling of being split in two, realize that this is a chance for reversing time and surfing the dragon lines of fate.

4. Maintain your old self and try to avoid or control what is happening.

5. When you no longer succeed, gather up courage and let your old identity and behavior change by letting yourself become the situation or feeling that is bothering you. Notice new parts of yourself that are now arising.

6. Begin to move, feel, and express yourself differently.

7. Look around. Notice the world's feedback. Notice how your body feelings and your relationships change. Watch the world around you and look for its synchronistic agreements.

8. In what way did you die and develop instead of getting annihilated?

NOTES

1. See Feynman, *Lectures in Physics.*
2. See Mindell, *Coma: Key to Awakening.*

CHAPTER 14

Awareness and Entropy

A useful theory not only must describe what has already been observed but also must be able to predict events to come. In these last chapters, I want to predict certain aspects of world-work, such as the reversal of time and the creation of order from chaos or negentropy.

The concepts and theory presented in the first part of this book generate attitudes and methods for working with world situations that make sense of nonlocal effects. Worldwork even hints at ways to enjoy seemingly chaotic or disturbing events. Field ideas allow for the possibility of time reversal.

What about future events? The word *future* is complicated. In terms of process work, *future* means nothing more than the hidden present, the disavowed or secondary processes happening right now. What is coming next can be foretold by that which is trying to happen in the moment. To find the future, therefore, we need to look at our feelings, symptoms, dreams, and double signals in relationships. To find the future at the global level, we need to examine our collective dreams, myths, and synchronicities.

Existing myths about the planet give us reason for pessimism. Some of the most well known myths about the globe predict the end of the world. For instance, the Chinese earth figure, Pan Ku, goes to pieces after creating himself as the world. The German myth of the Götterdämmerung is a horrible vision of death and destruction without rebirth.[1]

Self-Balance and Self-Destruction

Do these myths predict our future or point to the self-balancing tendency of nature of which I spoke in earlier chapters? Timespirits, left to themselves, can kill each other, just as matter collides with anti-matter, reality with dreams. Parts of a system will automatically balance and compensate for each other, resulting either in suicide and misery or in wisdom and wholeness, depending upon whether or not awareness plays a role.

For example, a client I once saw was suffering from hallucinations and was in a mental institution. He heard voices, and one voice, which identified itself as God, told him to kill a child. When he looked in the mirror, he saw a child smiling at him. Screaming that he had found the child, he put a gun to his head and killed the child, and thus himself.

This was an unsuccessful and self-destructive attempt at self-balancing. I knew this man and knew that he was resisting growing up. He actually was childish. Like many of us, he did not want to grow up and leave home, which in his case was the psychiatric clinic. The voice that told him to kill the child was an attempt to balance himself. He had one-sidedly nurtured the child and refused to support his adult tendencies. His suicide was a self-balancing act that led not to wisdom but to chaos.

At the global level, too, we are used to seeing self-balancing attempts that lead to destruction rather than wisdom. Groups tend to be one-sided and are thus inevitably opposed by other equally one-sided groups. Factions and individuals meet, threaten each other, and frequently try to kill each other. Done without awareness, compensating for a one-sided tendency leads more often to war and destruction than to wisdom and order. However, as we saw in the last chapter, what appears at first to be inner conflict or group conflict could also be a chance for self-discovery, for upsetting time and revealing the spaceless and timeless nature of life.

Entropic Destruction in Physics

In physics, the second law of thermodynamics mirrors the myths of destruction and predicts that the world will come to an end. The first law of thermodynamics says that the energy of the universe cannot be destroyed or created but can only be transformed. The second law of thermodynamics states that energy can be transformed into other forms and shift back again, but that a certain amount of available energy is lost every time such a transaction takes place. The total amount of energy remains the same, but its availability for doing practical work is lost in systems that are closed to outside interaction.

According to this theory, usually attributed to Clerk Maxwell, the whole universe, insofar as it is a closed system, is headed for "heat death," complete entropy or dissipation of useful energy. The energy in a closed system become less usable for work; thus, closed systems self-destruct. It is a matter of debate, however, whether the universe and the earth are truly closed systems, but the principle behind the second law will be important to us regardless.

Both mythology and physics seem to predict that our earth and closed systems in general are headed for destruction. I have asked hundreds of people around the world for their responses to the following two questions. First, do you think our planetary fate is to destroy ourselves? Second, what is the role of human beings, governments, or God in the face of entropy or planetary death?

I have heard various answers to these vast questions. Many say, "Yes, the world will die." Some say, "No, God will intervene." Still others say, "People will solve the problems."

Maxwell's Demon

My answer to the first question is yes and no. Yes, the world is obviously heading toward self-destruction as long as self-balance is not tempered by awareness, but no, the world need not destroy itself, which is the message of this book. Human beings may be able to reverse entropic processes through awareness.

Clerk Maxwell, too, posited a theory of reversing destructive entropic processes. It is not surprising, since the second law of thermodynamics is such a dismal world view, that Maxwell himself tried to balance it with a hypothesis that the law could be reversed if a little humanlike being, a demon, lived in the closed system and was able to regulate what happened. This demon is referred to as the Maxwellian demon.

According to Maxwell, a demon in a closed system could control the flow of molecules as they went back and forth between the two parts of the closed system. In a closed system, without a demon, hot molecules and cool molecules mix uncontrollably and eventually become a system of uniform temperature, a mixture incapable of doing work. The demon could reverse this, however. He could create "negentropy," which means that he could use the flow of molecules to generate a lot of useful work.

Analogously, if chemical reactions that raised the overall temperature were occurring in a system like the planet, the demon could use the increased heat to do work and thereby cool the planet without losing any of the potential for work. In other words, if there were a Maxwellian demon in the earth's system, and if it were a closed system, the demon could reverse the greenhouse effect—if, and only if, the demon's awareness were present.

Awareness and Energy

The world myths above predict, like the second law of thermodynamics, the destruction of the world because it lacks demons of awareness. Most anthropos myths are concerned with gods, not people. The laws of entropy, too, have no room for human consciousness and are therefore not influenced by subtle changes in our awareness. Without such awareness our sciences and myths are the same: both imply that the universe will destroy itself.

Scientists might argue that the universe or the earth is not really a closed system. However, the earth becomes a psychologically closed system more than we realize. These myths and laws describe a real and dangerous everyday process that we all know: the process of being locked into closed systems, unconscious situations without awareness. Science and mythology describe everyday reality as a closed system. They say nothing about what could happen in systems where someone is sufficiently detached to work with the polarizations!

A system without the demon of awareness is a world composed of individuals in altered states of consciousness, powerful emotional states such as ecstasy and depression, war and anger with no access to awareness and wisdom. How often do we all live in such closed system states, feeling things such as anger and depression without awareness?

All such states of consciousness that happen without awareness are closed and potentially destructive systems. Great discoveries, for example, the discovery of atomic energy, seem wonderful, yet without awareness of atomic energy's potential for murder, the world destroyed a large part of itself. When those of us who live in the West hear of the democratic revolutions happening in Eastern bloc countries, we feel relieved. But we need to maintain our awareness of the spirit of tyranny and power. If we only embrace freedom and leave out the timespirit of the tyrant, countries will simply flip toward freedom and have a violent and entropic reaction at another time. The unprocessed tyranny, power, and rage can sabotage the democratic movement.

History, Change, and Awareness

History has been the story of one revolution after another, one violent flip followed by another. Real change, however, is not flipping from one state to another without awareness. Flipping is merely replacing one timespirit with another, replacing democracy with totalitarianism, or replacing hate with love. We need a new history, a new world in which systems do not flip but are consciously facilitated in such a way that all parts are heard and one no longer simply overcomes the other.

Awareness does not mean discovering and bringing up new parts of ourselves that make war, that is, ones that break through and overcome old parts. This is not awareness. A psychology or worldwork that helps individuals discover new behaviors or new parts merely recharges us momentarily by giving us access to images and behavior that have been split off. I am calling for something more subtle. I am interested not in new growth but in the awareness process. This means that I am interested in the whole system, including the new parts, the older ones they are trying to replace, and the interaction between the old and the new. I am not interested in replacing the old tyrant with an eventual new one.

Awareness means that there is a Maxwellian demon, a facilitator standing in the otherwise closed system, enabling democracy and tyranny to know each other, use each other, and not just flip from one side to another. Awareness means not repressing power but using it with awareness. If we just flip from tyranny to democracy, power goes unconscious and turns up in hurtful ways! If we do not use awareness to mediate the relationship between timespirits, we will self-destruct by unconsciously balancing and flipping from one side to another. Thus, *it is not change that is essential, but the awareness of change, of what happens to the old parts during the change.*

If we are lucky, we will find a Maxwellian demon in the form of a family therapist, mediator, good friend, or adviser who will be with us in our closed systems to help us process things usefully. But when we are alone, this deeply democratic demon-therapist is usually missing.

Who of us is ready to use awareness, to take her own side with passion and awareness, to take her partner's side compassionately, and to stand clearly and neutrally outside the conflict, enabling both parts to interact within the limits of the heart and the mind?

Awareness implies understanding that what is opposing us is a part of ourselves that we need. Awareness often means reversing our minds, going backward, stepping outside the linear path we are on, and going with feelings and timespirits as they emerge within us. Awareness is related to sensing our own authoritarian position. Perhaps we can only learn to follow nature by first trying and failing to direct her according to what we have in our minds. Even the most benevolent procedures are doomed without a newer and deeper democracy requiring awareness in closed systems.

War is the most intense of all closed systems. There are two or more sides in conflict, each interested in overcoming the other, and no part with awareness. Our tendency to lock ourselves up in closed systems without awareness is why we frequently feel stuck on a planet without a leader. Too few of us are ready to reverse ourselves, to undergo the metaphorical death we are creating, and to temporarily abandon our identities and be guided by awareness.

Our greatest danger lies in our tendency to create a closed, unenlightened system that will balance itself to death. Until now, human history has cycled as new leaders, ideas, and groups merely overtake older ones, without reference to how this is done. As a group, we look like the individual: we grew up, rebelled, became adults, and repressed others! Likewise, as new global movements arise and crush older parties, most of us either take sides, suffer quietly, or passively read the newspapers. In the future we will be able to maintain our own autonomy only by being demons of awareness, reacting, making sure that change happens most humanely, by keeping in mind all parts and all people.

History turns and twists in its apparently inevitable struggle between creation and annihilation, while the majority of us sit back and imagine, "This is the natural course of history. It is too ancient and too immense for us to deal with." Or is it?

NOTE

1.   See Mindell, *The Year I,* for further references to planetary myths.

CHAPTER 15

Deep Democracy

As the millennium changes, we are beginning to agree that conflict and war have patterned history in part because we cling so stubbornly to our identities as individuals and groups. The second law of thermodynamics reflects ancient myths about our behavior, displaying worlds without consciousness drifting ruthlessly toward death. In our dark and closed emotional systems, we are either on this side or on that one. Science, myth, and just plain common sense forewarn us about self-destruction. Like the proverbial electron annihilated by its own double in an electromagnetic field or the world dying in its own greenhouse, we pretend that we are different from our opponents and behave as powerless beings at the mercy of volatile gods.

But science and mythology predict the chance for transforming. Like Feynman's awakened electron or Maxwell's demon of awareness, we can also temporarily step out of time and space, reverse entropy, and flow with nature. This alternative to heat death and the hothouse is a majestic vision of global transformation in which the world, like a self-healing shaman, steps out of time's linearity and processes its various roles. This vision must eventually succeed, because self-awareness, group awareness, and processing conflict are more thrilling than war and far more creative than peace.

Until now, this vision has only been a hopeful dream. Soon, however, it will be a wakeful necessity. But how? Knowing about fields and transnational groups and even practicing the worldwork tools described in this book are helpful and necessary but not sufficient. Neither the tools nor the theory alone will make things work any better than organizational ideas without the feeling of deep democracy.

Illness and Conflict

Reconsider the situation of the little boy with a brain tumor discussed in an earlier chapter. Remember how discipline appeared in his work? He had already been operated on twice when his parents brought him to me. They came to me thinking they had nothing more to lose. I asked the little boy how he experienced his tumor, and he said that it hurt him.

"How does it hurt?" I asked.

He said, "It hurts like a hammer." As he said the word *hammer*, he punched his knee. I asked him to hit his knee again and say "hammer" at the same time. He began hammering on his knee, with my encouragement, and we continued playfully hammering together until he knew the message in the hammer. After a minute or two, he looked at me a bit sheepishly and said the "hammer" told him to get to work, watch less television, and do his homework.

I helped him process this further by taking over the other side. Acting like the obstinate part of him, I complained that I liked television and did not want to do my homework. This made the boy go even further into the hammer's position. He insisted that "I" had to discipline myself. Finally we made a peace treaty. First the boy could do some homework; then he could watch a little television and then get back to work again.

The boy was happy with this decision. It gave him inner peace and more fun in life through the experience of being a hammer. His mother, however, was not pleased. She was convinced that he was in too much pain to study. The boy and I "hammered" away at her, yelling boisterously that he wanted more discipline! We all laughed, and she supported the child to do his homework.

The boy's health improved radically. Eventually he felt completely better. Later his doctor told me that the X rays showed that the tumors had vanished. Even more important was the boy's joy at being tougher. But what had reversed the destruction process? Luck?

I think that Maxwell's demon got inside the boy. Up until the moment when the conflict became conscious, he had been living in a psychologically closed system that was trying to balance itself. On one side of the system was a normal lazy kid, and on the other was a very industrious, disciplined person who wanted to study. The two were killing each other, and there was no one "home" to mediate their conflict.

Self-Balance vs. Awareness

The self-balancing nature of the child alone would have killed him. This is what some myths and the laws of physics predict. But a mediator who could step into that closed system, who could separate and combine the discipline and television processes, allowed the conflict to result in both more homework and more television. Best of all, it permitted the child to live.

Let us examine this mediation process in detail. Before mediation began, there were two timespirits in conflict, the hammer and the lazy television viewer. The hammer was killing both itself and the television viewer in the form of a brain tumor. When awareness entered the scene, however, the boy became aware of the tumor's message, became attracted to the energy behind discipline, and could also appreciate the television viewer! Finally, there were no sides at all in conflict, and excitement reigned.

One side never wins alone in human systems. There are no sustainable solutions in which one person or spirit represses another. Moreover, permanent conflict resolutions are no more realizable than is ending all headaches with one aspirin. Therefore, a viable worldwork must at least show the existence and value of all sides and also allow us the transporting experience of appreciating and living each side as it arises, one after the other.

The feeling that nourishes this experience is therefore more than democracy, more than the hope for peace and conflict resolution. It is a deeper democracy that respects not only each part but also its capacity to make us whole. When people have this attitude, apparently destructive processes like the child's may became as exciting and useful as they are dangerous.

This child not only got better; he also experienced his life as richer and more fun. Deep democracy inspires us to recycle aspects of ourselves we would throw away. I have shown many times in this book that recycling destructive conflict and toxic contempt does not simply mean resolution; it can mean personal wholeness, more community, and enthusiasm for all.

The Global Future

As we discover and experiment with timespirits, combining, inter-
acting, and identifying with them, everyone and everything experiences increased meaning, insight, and enlightenment. The minimum
result is that the invisible elements clogging up the atmosphere clearly
appear for all to see. This visibility stirs us all and provokes us to
respond to social issues. Sometimes, momentary improvements in our
world situation follow. What appears from one viewpoint to be a disas-
trous problem, illness, or conflict unfolds from another viewpoint and
reveals itself as an awesome opportunity.

Such work makes life more worthwhile, but how far can it go? Will
it also heal illness and save the world? Yes and no. Yes, the theory about
the nonlocal aspect of our personal lives predicts that individual awareness is linked to global effects. And no, problems and conflicts are like
dreams, forever recreating themselves, challenging us with new situations and potentials for development until we become completely fluid.

Just as global problems are connected to individual awareness, the
healing of our individual symptoms may depend in part upon the consciousness of others. Family work has long demonstrated how an
adult's development may relieve an infant's symptoms. Therefore, we
must remain open to the fact that certain individual, group, and earth
problems cannot clear up without global changes in many of us. In this
way, any one individual's problems are global. The field in which we
live influences our dreams and bodies.

New Myths and Awareness

The way to better health is the same as the way to a more sustainable politics. Good health requires Maxwellian awareness and the fluidity of a spiritual warrior in the midst of personal trouble. By sensing
and separating the timespirits of a field, we reorganize their meeting,
avoid their annihilation, and dissolve and pick up their energies.
Worldwork is a new myth where human beings intervene where earlier
only gods existed.

Awareness, the perennial concern of many traditions such as Zen,
vipassana, Taoism, and the martial arts, will play a decisive role in the
world of the future. Awareness will become an even more important
and differentiated catchword as we realize its potential for cocreating
history. In the past, awareness signified for many people a relatively

neutral or passive state of consciousness. Now it means objective alertness that notices inner experiences and outer events but can also lead to emptiness and free, creative action. It means openness to ourselves and others and also the capacity to temporarily enter any one of the streams of life. It means remembering our whole selves in the midst of chaos, listening to the voices of those we like, and also experimenting with becoming our seemingly impossible opponents.

Above all, awareness will not be limited to individual life but will characterize the group mind as well. We need highly evolved people and completely awake organizations in which everyone participates, knowing when to be quiet or noisy, joining in the mad cacophony of voices and at the same time capable of detaching from the compelling nature of the field. This new awareness has many options to it. We can passively observe events, try to control them, be at their service, and also use them to discover our awesomeness.

Such changes in our concept of awareness will not leave global events or the laws of physics untouched. As we learn to conflict, serve, and care for the spirits moving within our clogged environment, negentropy effects will occur. This could mean that we shall live through a period of miracles. Previous laws of physics, for example, the second law of thermodynamics, which were based upon the assumption that there was no consciousness in closed systems, must be relativized or fall from the Olympian heights of dogmatic teachings. Even "modern" quantum physics could become an outmoded fairy tale of the sleeping human race, which suddenly awoke to its potential of cocreating history. The science of matter will no longer be separable from the study of consciousness.

And what about our physiology? Until now, our minds and bodies have felt like the battlefields we read about in the newspapers. Personal work, caring for unconscious states such as haste and drowsiness, will certainly contribute to leading a more meaningful existence and perhaps even increase the length of life. Extrapolating into physiology, consciously processing and riding malignant tensions like waves on the sea may free our bodies and earth from being the stage for the war between global timespirits. The anatomy of our internal organs, which now seem built to handle so much tension, will change. If we channel the earth's quakes, droughts, and animal and plant voices, our bodies might become more sensitive and open up to new experiences that are presently beyond our imagination.

We have the threat of unsolvable ecological problems and the end of life on earth to thank for provoking us to awaken to our total potential.

Regardless of their beliefs, everyone I have worked with who was near death has been challenged by mortality to realize their greatest gifts, open up, and follow the flow of things. Everyone near death seems to become a Taoist. Our new myths must tell the awesome tale of how we almost suffocated while moving between centuries. Yet we awakened from our closed planetary system and were saved from near extinction by learning how to reverse entropy and utilize conflicts and tensions for creativity.

Planetary negentropy can be connected with time reversal and may coincide with increased psychic and telepathic ability. As the indigenous tribes of the Third World succumb to economic pressures and the allure of high-tech, the shaman, wise person, and healer will be reborn in everyone's increasing sensitivity and knowledge about fields. We do not need many such wise shamanic figures, but we certainly need more who mediate between the spirits and people in our renewed global tribe.

Thus theory predicts that changes in consciousness can reverse the entropy law and the earth's destruction or at least recreate some of our lost natural resources from the energy locked up in our choking greenhouse. I hope the momentary breakthroughs and mind and time reversals implied by worldwork theory will encourage many. But I also expect these possibilities to drive those few already close to heaven into god-intoxicated states, even though such New Age glows are merely light dreams compensating for the media's doomsday presentations. As the euphoric glow of hope wanes when facing the problems of today, we shall understand our dreams of peace on earth and freedom from hunger and grief as potentials that will work only when we accept the energy behind brutality and process belligerence.

Deep Democracy

In a world threatened by heat death, "good" and "bad" become less important than the relationship between them. Our conscious experience of both determines whether we gain or lose. The next global step cannot be just a remodeled religion where "being nice" prevails. The spark of the Maxwellian demon promises a life that is more complete than a heaven without hell.

Worldwork begins wherever there is an attitude toward life that encompasses the transforming whole and is ecologically minded. It occurs whenever we begin by fighting to win and ends by accepting and facilitating our chaos. There are so many people interested in a new way of living on earth that worldwork is not only a national but also a transnational political party occupied by everyone who wants more than majority rule. Worldwork facilitators want more connection to themselves and relationship between all parties in their groups.

Today, the United Nations is perhaps the most prominent peace-making forum we have for crisis. The UN has thirty-two organs to watch over our global health, peace, literacy, nourishment, and industry. Yet the UN, our sole global facilitating body, is less than fifty years old. Before 1948, no one knew how many people lived on earth because we did not have the statistics! Today, for the first time in history, overpopulation is being checked.

However, the UN should not be the only world body responsible for global thinking and capable of considering the world's problems interdependently. Each of us and each of our organizations are responsible for the global field. This means that we consider daily questions we normally encounter only at the end of life, such as what the meaning of our personal existence is. We should ponder global, existential, and profound questions. What is our role on earth right now? What is fate asking our group to do?

Individual psychology and organizational awareness are worldwork. What we do in this moment impinges on the world. Our feelings and emotions are the feelings of a world part trying to get along with other parts. The way we get along with ourselves administrates the world's development. Since innerwork is worldwork, we are creating a psychologically based political view that values and facilitates the connection between the parts and spirits of the environment.

Democracy is a good beginning name for this view, but we need more than public elections and New Age attempts at leaderless groups. We need new forms that encourage understanding of ourselves and work with opposing parties. We need an updated anarchy, a renewed democracy, to create a party that is an open circle, a time-spirit that can be entered by anyone for a moment and then left again when it no longer fits. We need a party and politics that reflect a deeper democracy.

Deep democracy touches upon all levels of our lives. In personal life, it means openness to all of our inner voices, feelings, and movements, not just the ones we know and support, but also the ones we fear and do not know well. In relationships, deep democracy means having ongoing awareness of our highest ideals and worst moods. In group life it means the willingness to listen to and experiment with whatever part comes up. In global work, deep democracy values politics, ethnicity, separatism, and the spirit of nature.

Deep democracy itself is an ancient idea that comes and goes in all of us whenever sensitivity is used in connection to fields and groups. This sensitivity involves awareness, earthservice, and representation.

Awareness. Interest in ourselves, others, and outer events contributes to the global field's wisdom. If we notice what is happening, we can use its energies consciously. There can be no democracy without awareness and acceptance of all our internal and external parts.

Earthservice. Deep democracy supports the experiences of native peoples who treat the earth as if it were a human being with power and magic. We realize that whatever we do involves the nature of a certain locality, and that we must respect and allow that piece of earth into our awareness through direct environmental intervention and through representing the earthspirit in our group processes by people who love it. We need to pick up plastic and also play out the conflict between the one who dropped it and the soil it hurts.

Deep democracy is awareness that the world can only partially be understood. Its inexplicable nature leads us to interact with the mysterious powers of the field in which we live.

Representation. Deep democracy is based upon the realization that everyone is needed to represent reality. Since deep democracy is an idea, it can appear anywhere and anytime in any group as a feeling or belief. We all belong to the deep democracy party when we are touched by its timespirit. In principle, it should boast the greatest membership of any party, since everyone belongs to it at one time or another. Yet it has no fixed membership, for no one can permanently belong to such a state of loving compassion.

Sadly enough, in spite of its great potential, the spirit of deep democracy itself is one of the least populated parts of our world. We all tend to be prejudiced and undemocratic. We support only normal polarities of good and bad politics and accept only known or "good" parts of ourselves. Then we flip and become possessed by newly emerging forces. Or we act statically neutral and aloof.

Deep democracy is different. It stands for itself and all the other parties as well. It does not forget the times before revolutions but tries to find some value in both the old and the new without identifying with either. Deep democracy knows that the past automatically becomes an influential ghost in the present and therefore tries to usefully embody the energy of apparently dead, repressed, even tyrannical spirits.

Elders in the City

There are more than enough of these spirits to remember. Consider city crime. We spend too much time policing people and not enough time finding sustainable solutions. To work with city violence, we need to improve the situation of the poor and also recognize gifted young people, who naturally model the facilitation skills of deep democracy. They could do that kind of worldwork that transforms the energy of violence into liveliness and community.

Consider civil rights. The way minority groups are dealt with around the world is humiliating and inhuman. We need new laws to enforce civil rights but also a new concept of what it means to be human, for laws alone will not be obeyed where prejudice exists. We need more than laws, lawyers, politicians,.and military leaders; we need tribal elders. Where are our wise women and men, boys and girls who parent one another, encouraging us to admit and process our fear and love for others?

Our earliest tribal leaders combined spiritual and mundane characteristics. Now that tribal life is dying out, a new eldership role will arise that must be shared by everyone. We need to search within and outside for these elders and support anyone we find who models the principles of deep democracy. Part of our global work is to find and love this wise aspect of ourselves. Our next leaders will be not only those charismatic few who are courageous enough to stand up in public but also those who quietly model the eldership role at home.

These elders are as important as democratic governments in caring for us, as we find our inner selves and live with others of different religions, races, gender, and economic privileges. We must have more jobs for the poor, improve housing conditions, and give aid to street people, but we must also enable the rich and the poor to relate to each other. The way in which democracy and capitalism are practiced today does not help, because present leaders do not understand depression, suicide, and the sense of meaninglessness that so many feel.

And drugs? Elders who have experienced their own altered states of consciousness know that laws and police are not going to heal drug addictions. We need to get deeper into forbidden trance states and find the crucial secrets we have lost there. We addict ourselves to aspects of life not allowed in the present world. We need leaders who have a sense of deep democracy and who can help us find the energy and life we are looking for in the altered states of consciousness that drugs bring.

What about government deceit? The elder knows herself and realizes that neither increased prosperity nor moral proscriptions will ever stop stealing and lying. Everyone wants to be appreciated and secretly steals, at least in the sense of covertly eliciting love and encouragement. When governments do not encourage full participation from everyone at all levels of work, stealing from the state becomes a central news topic, as it is in many modern countries. The elder practicing deep democracy, however, brings the timespirit of the criminal outlaw forward. She embraces it in order to fulfill its deepest needs: creativity and empowerment.

We cannot go on fooling ourselves into thinking that the world can be run by politicians and leaders who are not elders. The only sustainable solutions to problems are ones containing at least as much love and human understanding as law and order.

The environment too cannot be saved by rules alone. As soon as conflict arises between two countries, the weaker one will destroy the environment to terrorize the stronger. We need national leaders who are transnational martial artists as well as ecologists. Elders practicing deep democracy will expect and even invite disturbers into the circle before they become terrorists. These leaders embrace the wild ones, making terrorism obsolete by opening up social agendas and considering even unpopular ideas.

Sustainable, viable leadership means elders who are politically wise, psychologically oriented people interested in personal development as well as everything else. We will always need charismatic, inspirational leaders. However, even more we need compassionate people who have feelings that go beyond right and wrong and the borders of their own person and nation and are capable of understanding and helping others.

The Elders' Problems

As we grow into becoming elders, we need encouragement as we fumble along. Modeling deep democracy may sometimes be as difficult as it is awe inspiring. Genuine eldership cannot be an act, for it is not enough to behave openly to others. If we do not realize and admit our prejudices at least to ourselves, others will feel them. There are no longer any secrets in our post-Einsteinian universe, in which mental telepathy is as important as fax machines. Everyone knows everything.

Unconscious unprocessed prejudice creates insidious, invisible conflicts. However, if we realize our prejudices, we can enter consciously into conflict with outer events. Only when we know our opinions can we let go of them for a moment and listen to others. Such consciousness can be difficult, however, especially in the midst of turbulent power struggles. Today, as countries strive for freedom and independence, everyone everywhere is struggling to create a new world order. As old, non-process-oriented forms of leadership fail, groups and nations face the challenge but also agony of creating deeper democracies than we have had in the past.

Chaos reigns during these times of transition, as everyone seems to battle everyone else. Various leaders fight for power, and the wise elders seem to be missing. Where is the elder now who supports one side and then all others? The one who can seem as crazy as everyone else in the mob but can also detach herself from the turmoil of emerging leaders in order to listen quietly and actively to each and every one, giving them all—including herself—the consideration they deserve.

If she knows herself well, she remembers that even her love for peace and harmony can create conflict. When she is awake, she clearly stands for her ideals and then lets them go as her mind focuses upon the reality of the moment and the development of everyone. Even if she goes unconscious for moments, her central intent is more important: remembering those of us who are still unborn as well as herself.

Ghandi's magnificent story of facilitating India's independence from the British Commonwealth has much to teach. His inspirational nonviolence saved the moment but also repressed the timespirit of brutality that killed him and possessed India for some time thereafter. Our twenty-first-century elders must simultaneously be violent, nonviolent, and neither.

Egalitarian communities, the idealistic dream of the 1960s, did not work because of powerful capitalistic systems and also because the powerful people in leaderless groups could not get along together. This is why today alternative groups have so little power: they cannot reach a consensus. Democracy works only with consciousness, when participants know their own views, allow conflict with others, and have access to the sense of eldership that is beyond any momentary opinion.

When the elder realizes that she cannot control or overcome the chaotic storms of leaders vying for power, she can still discover the magic of deep democracy, and the impossible always seems to get done. Only when we are exhausted from trying to control the controllers can we use the tools of worldwork. Then everyone relaxes, and the world falls mysteriously into order again, if only for a moment.

Thus, without deep democratic training and know-how, revolution that overthrows old systems to create newer and better ones will repeat the past. Governmental structures alone will not bring about a deep democracy. Only individual awareness can do that, for no system exists without at least subtle hierarchies. We must have the courage to make power visible and stand for it. Then others can accept or combat it, and, best of all, awareness will suggest that we can leave our position when others arise who do it better.

Unlike some philosophies and belief systems, deep democracy begins by admitting that it is incapable of saving anyone or anything. It may solve some conflicts and problems, but only when the time has come for everyone involved to utilize their energy personally in relationships and in organizations. The power and success of deep democracy depend entirely upon the awareness of the processes at hand. Thus, the spirit of deep democracy supports neither the use of power in politics nor the preaching of peace, but rather encourages awareness of them both as they appear in the moment. It does not know what to do. Though it tries for solutions, it trusts none, since as we all know, everything changes.

Since no one is a perfect elder, there will be times when the facilitator fails to appreciate the opponents in conflict. In those agonizing moments, both the oppressor and the oppressed may join in accusing her of creating worlds that are unsafe or are open forums for trouble. She has no choice but to agree and apologize for her unconsciousness. For no one feels endangered when the elder's awareness is present. Then aggressive parties are allowed to be angry but are also encouraged to notice their fear, sadness, and quiet. Even the silent parties will be happy if they are appreciated for being withdrawn and meditative or encouraged to come forward and criticize as their signals imply.

The only unsafe group is a closed one, a world in which awareness of change is not present. Thus, we elders in training survive attack and misunderstanding by growing and praying that others will soon help in occupying our position. Then, before the authorities accuse us of being the advocate of the underdogs, we can notice that these authorities are not the paradigm of evil everyone thought but are also insecure or even sensitive about hurting others. They need support like everyone else in tense systems if they are to leave their positions or meet the attacks coming their way.

If the elder is quick, she will advise the minority that her apparent and momentary support of its opponents is really more than that. She is nourishing the seeds of the only viable government, deep democracy and awareness. Doubting questions from the minority, however, might indicate that she has forgotten a part of herself, the site from which she sprang long ago, her own sense of impotence and disempowerment, pain, and anger. She was never really an objective observer after all, for she remembers that the roots of today's action came from ancient visions of a better world, a fire that kindled hope long before her time and will continue to illuminate global change after she is gone.

So when the minority asks, "What about immediate, concrete changes, more time, money, and appreciation?" she will answer, "Yes, let us go for them all and much, much more."

Large systems are like people: both need structural change, patience, and healing. There are no quick or permanent fixes for anything today. Yet we must not wait for our gigantic systems or the whole of ourselves to shift from torpor to activity. Patience must not cover up our ability to provoke but should center us in disturbing the world around us to change, transmuting international problems and personal illnesses into enjoyment and satisfaction. We have no time to wait even for our own eldership to emerge but must experiment now in working with networks and individuals. Our good intent and effort will awaken the slumbering wisdom of others and experiences that surpass momentary solutions, war, or even peace.

The news confronts each of us daily with planetary adversaries, timespirits deadlocked in combat. Our present international legal and political systems are overwhelmed by processes which are beyond determination of the "the truth," who is right and who is wrong. The elder in us all knows that there is no final equity in blunt adversarial conflict. A sense of justice arises only in connection with community, with inner peace of mind, sustainable ongoing relationships, and worldwork that processes the tension between groups.

There is no succeeding or failing with deep democracy. It knows neither winning nor losing, neither inside nor out, neither Yin nor Yang, but is deeper and more fundamental. Its focus is upon the swirling cycles that create the wholeness we call the world. Some hope that this focus will emerge in the figure of a new elder who has been missing in our global tribe. Others experience such focus as their own capacity to love, which appreciates and facilitates all the elements of change.

Bibliography

Ackerman, Linda. "Managing Flow State." *Newsletter of Association for Human Psychology*, 1986.

Allen, R. F., and C. Kraft. *The Organizational Unconscious*. Englewood Cliffs, NJ: Prentice-Hall, 1982.

Belfore-Wilson, Maria. "Archetype in a Group Experience." *Pratt Institute of Creative Arts Therapy Review* 3 (1982): 41–48.

Bertalanffy, Ludwig von. *General Systems Theory*. New York: Braziller, 1968.

Bohm, David. *Unfolding Meaning*. London and New York: Ark Paperbacks, 1985.

Bradford, David L., and Allen Cohen. *Managing for Excellence*. New York: Wiley, 1984.

Briggs, John, and F. David Peat. *Turbulent Mirror: An Illustrated Guide to Chaos Theory and the Science of Wholeness*. New York: Harper & Row, 1989.

Campbell, Joseph. *The Power of Myth*. New York: Doubleday, 1988.

Capra, Fritjof. *Uncommon Wisdom: Conversations with Remarkable People*. New York: Simon & Schuster, 1988.

Castaneda, Carlos. *Journey to Ixtlan*. New York: Simon & Schuster, 1971.

Clancy, John J. *Invisible Powers*. Lexington, MA: Lexington, 1989.

Davis, S. M. "Transforming Organizations: The Key to Strategy Is Context." *Organizational Dynamics* (Winter 1982): 64–68.

Devos, George Hsu, L. K. Francis, and Anthony J. Marsella, eds. *Culture and Self: Asian and Western Perspectives*. New York: Tavistock, 1985.

Dunningan, James F., and Austin Bay. *A Quick and Dirty Guide to War: Briefings on Present and Potential Wars*. New York: William Morrow, 1985.

Dworkin, Jan. "Group Process Work: A Stage for Personal and Global Development." Unpublished dissertation, Union Institute, Cincinnati, OH, 1989.

Dyer, William G. *Team Building*. Reading MA: Addison-Wesley, 1989.

Faber, M. D. *Culture and Consciousness: The Social Meaning of Altered Awareness*. New York: Human Science Press, 1981.

Feynman, Richard. "The Theory of Positrons." *Physical Review* 76, no. 6 (1949).

———. *Lectures in Physics*. New York: Addison-Wesley, 3 vols. 1963–65.

Goodbread, Joseph. *The Dreambody Toolkit.* New York: Viking-Penguin, 1987.

Goodman, Howard. "Give War a Chance." *Philadelphia Inquirer,* June 19, 1987.

Grof, Stanislav. "Perinatal Roots of Wars, Totalitarianism, and Revolutions: Observations from LSD Research." *Revision* 8, no. 1 (1985).

Hamman, Jamil. "A Moderate Solution." *Newsweek,* Aug. 16, 1982.

Hanh, Thich Naht. *Being Peace.* Berkeley, CA: Parallax Press, 1988.

Harman, Willis. *Global Mind Change: The Promise of the Last Years of the Twentieth Century.* Indianapolis: Knowledge Systems, 1988.

Hawking, Stephen W. *A Brief History of Time.* New York: Bantam Books, 1988.

Jung, C. G. *The Collected Works.* Vol. 14, *Mysterium Coniunctionus.* London: Routledge and Kegan Paul, 1978.

Kanter, Rosabeth M. *The Change Masters.* New York: Simon & Schuster, 1983.

Lamb, David. *The Africans.* New York: Vintage, 1987.

McGregor, Douglas. *The Human Side of Enterprise.* New York: McGraw-Hill, 1960.

Maslow, Abraham H. *The Farther Reaches of Human Nature.* New York: Viking Press, 1971.

Mindell, Amy. "Moon in the Water. Meta-Skills of Process Oriented Psychology." Unpublished doctoral dissertation, Union Institute, Cincinnati, OH, 1991.

Mindell, Amy, and Arnold Mindell. *Riding the Horse Backwards.* London and New York: Viking-Penguin, 1992.

Mindell, Arnold. *Dreambody, The Body's Role in Revealing the Self.* Boston: Sigo Press, 1982. London and New York: Viking-Penguin-Arkana, 1986.

———. *River's Way.* New York and London: Viking-Penguin-Arkana, 1985.

———. *Working with the Dreaming Body.* New York and London: Viking-Penguin-Arkana, 1986.

———. *The Dreambody in Relationships.* New York and London: Viking-Penguin-Arkana, 1987.

———. *City Shadows: Psychological Interventions in Psychiatry.* New York and London: Viking-Penguin-Arkana, 1988.

———. *Coma: Key to Awakening.* Boston, MA: Shambhala, 1989.

———. *Working on Yourself Alone.* New York and London: Viking-Penguin-Arkana, 1989.

———. *The Year I: Global Process Work with Planetary Myths and Structures.* New York and London: Viking-Penguin-Arkana, 1989.

Mirvis, Philip. "Work in the Twentieth Century." *Revision* 7, no. 2 (1984).

Netanyahu, Benjamin, ed. *Terrorism: How the West Can Win.* New York: Avon Books, 1986.

Nevis, Edwin C. *Organizational Consulting: A Gestalt Approach.* New York: Gardner Press, 1987.

Nunez, Antonio. *Organizational Transformation: The Emergence of a New Paradigm.* California Institute of Integral Studies, 1988.

Porras, Jerry I. Gayton E. Germane, ed. *Organizational Development. The Executive Course. What Every Manager Needs to Know about the Essentials of Business.* Reading, MA: Addison-Wesley, 1989.

Rogers, Carl. *On Encounter Groups.* New York: Harper & Row, 1970.

———. *On Personal Power.* New York: Delacorte, 1977.

Sheldrake, Rupert. "Extended Mind, Power and Prayer." *Psychological Perspectives* 19, no. 1 (1988).

Spurr, John. "Co-Dependence: A Process Oriented Developmental Approach." Unpublished dissertation, Institute of Transpersonal Psychology, Menlo Park, CA, 1989.

Stevens, Anthony. *The Roots of War: A Jungian Perspective.* New York: Paragon House, 1989.

Swan, James A. *Sacred Places.* Santa Fe, NM: Bear, 1989.

Thompson, William Irwin. *Pacific Shift.* San Francisco: Sierra Club Books, 1985.

Ueshiba, Kisshomaru. *The Spirit of Aikido.* Translated by Taitetsu Unno. Tokyo and New York: Kodansha International, 1988.

Yanoov, Benyaman. *The Pursuit of Peace: A Curriculum Manual for Junior and Senior High School Teachers.* Partnership, P.O. Box 95777, Haifa, Israel, 31095, 1985.

Index